AWAKE TO LIFE!
(Sermons from the Paschal (Easter) Cycle)

by Fr. Alexander Men

Foreword by
Bishop SERAPHIM (Sigrist)

Introduced by Fr. Michael Fortunato
Translated by Marite Sapiets

ΩAKWOOD ΠUBLICATIONS

First English Edition published by Bowerdean Press Ltd.,
London (1992)
Russian Edition by Natalia Grigorenko (1990)

U.S. Edition © 1996, with permission
ISBN 1-879038-26-9
ΩAKWOOD ΠUBLICATIONS
3827 Bluff Street
Torrance, California 90505-6359
(310) 378-9245 (OFFICE & FAX)
CompuServe Address: 71552,3164
Internet Address: 71552.3164@compuserve.com

Other Related Books by Oakwood Publications:

The Biography of Alexander Men (Yves Hamant) 1995
Conversations on the Church (Alexander Men) 1996
Son of Man (Alexander Men) 1996
Place of the Heart: Introduction to Orthodox Spirituality
(Elisabeth Behr-Sigel) 1992

Cover Design: Victoria Graphics, Orange, California
Printed in the USA by KNI, Inc., Anaheim, California

FOREWORD

This collection of Fr. Alexander Men's sermons, now available in an American edition, is the first of his works to be translated into English. It is peculiarly appropriate that this first available work be a book of sermons, because the sermon is the medium of communication for a pastor to his community, and Father Men was, first of all, a pastor.

He was, however, no ordinary pastor; his church at Knave Derevnia, in the suburbs of Moscow, became the center of a community of thousands who had been drawn to the Faith by his ministry.   In the later years of his work, until his assassination in 1990, Fr. Alexander was becoming a sort of pastor to the entire nation of Russia, as it emerged from the communist period. His spiritual friends and disciples included Alexander Solzhenitsyn and Andre Sakharov. His voice went out over television and radio, and his many books covered a range from a scholarly seven-volume study of the history of religions, to clear and simple explanations of all aspects of the Faith, to books for children. In the same way, among his followers, professors and students rubbed shoulders with ordinary people of all sorts and conditions.

Today, five years after his death, the community of spiritual children of Fr. Alexander goes on, and even spreads. In the way that one, perhaps, cannot speak of St. Francis without speaking of the early Franciscans, and yet also cannot speak of the Franciscans without going back to St. Francis, so here the man, Fr. Alexander, and the community of his spiritual children, are somehow inseparable. So Dr. Krister Sairsingh, preaching as chaplain at Harvard a year after Fr. Men's death, would say that, since nothing then was available in English, he could not approach Fr. Alexander through his books, but that, "...today I want to remember him, because his spiritual children have touched my life in ways I can hardly begin to describe." The sermons, then, stand at the point where Fr. Men and the people he pastored meet, and illuminate both the pastor and that still-vibrant and growing community.

These sermons were preached in the years between 1976 and 1989. Most of them are from 1988 and 1989, and they are from the season of Lent and Easter, through Pentecost, and, on one important level, form a valuable companion to the journey, through the heart of the Christian, specifically the Eastern Orthodox, liturgical year. If this were all, it would still be much. However, I believe as we read, and in effect listen to, these words--for as music resides eternally in the score, so a written sermon is forever speaking --I believe we will find more. One hearer of these sermons recalls that they were always like "a wave of life-giving energy and consolation. He showed us how, in spite of all problems, we would be able to give, because God gives us the real life." Furthermore, whatever the weather was when we went to Liturgy, somehow "...it was another miracle that we could see there at Knave Derevnia, that when we came out it was always sunny!" Another hearer recalls that when Fr. Alexander would speak before a time of confession, it was never in set phrases or spiritual clichés, but went to the heart, so that hearer after hearer, when the time came to speak to Fr. Alexander in private, would say, "...thank you , Father; you have already said everything." Now, the reader also joins the ranks of hearers of these sermons, and I believe that many will find that the words go to the heart of personal concerns and problems, and also come with a life-giving assurance of the absolute reality of God's Love and the availability of Divine guidance and strength.

Because is it not the real secret of Fr. Men, and of the people he gathered, that through both the teacher and the disciples one is drawn inexorably to Christ and to God alone? So one disciple observed, that since Fr. Alexander always referred everything to God, precisely for that reason we were able to go on with strength and joy after his death.

As more of his books become available in English, readers will be able to appreciate more of the depth and range of this great contemporary Christian teacher. He was completely a Russian Orthodox priest and teacher, and yet, so deeply had he drawn from the Gospels, he is one of those few who, without any loss of particularity or any unfaithfulness to their tradition, can speak absolutely for all Christians. Is it not for this reason that so many who know little or nothing of Anglicanism respond so immediately to the works of C.S.Lewis? So Fr. Men's work, which built bridges between Christianity and culture over which a generation of Russians could pass, may well provide bridges and ways forward for Christians far from Russia.

But first, at the beginning, let us stand in a modest country church, amid the flickering candles and the radiant icons, aware around us of a great crowd of young and old, artists, technicians, scientists, the unlettered together with the learned. Some have come from a great distance, and surely so have we; some have had a difficult journey, and perhaps ours has been, too. But now nothing matters except the joyful possibility to hear the Word of God and to see our lives in the Light of that Word.

Bishop SERAPHIM Joseph Sigrist, (Orthodox Bishop, formerly of Sendai and East Japan)

Preparation for Lent

Introduction

*The liturgical season, which the sermons in this collection illus-
trate, spans over eighteen Sundays, with the feast of Easter as its
theological centre. The theme of Christ's resurrection is present in
the worship of all these Sundays. New Testament readings are
prescribed for them, and they form the subject of most sermons in
this book. Many of the Gospel readings lend their names to the
Sundays concerned.*

*This period is centred on the idea of personal repentance. The
'beloved prayer' of repentance mentioned in the first sermon,
unfolds thus:*

> *"Open unto me, O Giver of life, the gates of repentance: for
> early in the morning my spirit seeks Thy holy temple, bearing
> a temple of the body all defiled. But in Thy compassion
> cleanse it by Thy loving kindness and mercy.*

> *'Guide me in the paths of salvation, O Mother of God: for I
> have befouled my soul with shameful sins and have wasted all
> my life in slothfulness. By Thine intercessions deliver me
> from all defilement.*

> *'Have mercy upon me, O God, in Thy great mercy: and
> according to the multitude of Thy tender mercies blot out my
> transgressions.*

1

'As I ponder in my wretchedness my many evil deeds I tremble in the fear of the day of judgement. But trusting in Thy merciful compassion, like David, do I cry to Thee: have mercy upon me, O God, in Thy great mercy".

These prayers continue to be sung at Matins on all Sundays during this period and also throughout Lent. They are normally sung slowly and with great intensity, impressing their message on the minds and hearts of the faithful.

This period begins soon after the coldest weeks of the Russian winter: no wonder that many funerals occur then (p.3/14). It is also the time of a more austere food diet: meat is given up at the close of the Sunday of the Last Judgement, until Easter Sunday; the week of Carnival follows (p.15). All fats, butter and cooking oils, as well as fish disappear from the tables on the evening of the Sunday of Forgiveness, as Lent begins in earnest the following morning.

In his sermon on the Last Judgement, (p.18) Fr. Alexander points to an icon representing Christ victorious, descending to Hell and shattering its defences, to rescue Adam and Eve from the grave. It is to the story of the fall of Adam that the last Sunday before the beginning of Lent is dedicated, when our forefather is described as sitting outside Paradise, weeping. On that same evening, a ritual of mutual forgiveness is enacted in the parishes after Vespers, inaugurating Lent.

Open unto me, O Giver of Life, the Gates of Repentance

In the name of the Father and of the Son and of the Holy Spirit!

The words of the canticle we all love still echo in our ears; "Open unto me, O Giver of Life, the Gates of Repentance". So Lent draws near.

As a traveller, approaching a river after a long journey, senses how cool the water will be, so you and I are getting nearer to the great time of purification. We should greet every Lent as if it were the last in our lives, so that we stop and think - if only for a short while, tearing ourselves away from the perpetual bustle and rush that constitutes our lives. Look how we live nowadays: how bitter and exhausted we are, what an endless hurry we are in - we're making such an effort, trying to make progress. But all of it comes to an end earlier than we realise. Here among us we already have someone who has left his abode - his body - and perhaps before we reach Lent, one of us might be lying here, like him, in the middle of the church.

Let us think for a while about how we can open up our souls to the Lord, how we can start to live a real life. So what kind of life is a "real life"? It is a life of love - for God and men - a life in which what is most important comes first and is not pushed aside by trivialities. When we stand before God, it is as though we are standing in front of a bright light, which shows up our unworthiness, our meanness and weakness. Before the face of God we are revealed as destitute. For the Lord is love, which He pours out on us. How can we thank Him, other than by returning that love? But, we ourselves do not possess it: we only see, in the light of the Divine Glory, how unworthy of it we are. God's Law,

3

according to the Apostle Paul, reveals and exposes our mortality and sinfulness.

What then can we men do? What kind of will-power, what exertions can free us from sin? You and I are no longer children and we understand very well that such efforts are largely useless. We return again and again to the same petty, boring, everyday sins: irritability, despondency, gloom, envy, vanity and malice conquer us in the same old way. Who will lead us out of this blind alley? Who can pull us out of the swamp in which our souls are stuck fast and perishing? We have no help or salvation other than the Lord Jesus Christ and His love - His extra love. His first love created us, giving life to us and to the world. But His extra love saw that we were incapable of making use of this, that we put everything good to evil purposes and live in an evil way. So His extra love stretches out a hand to us, saying "Arise, thou that sleepest, awake, awake....I, your Lord, have come to you. Although I was immortal, yet I died. I have experienced all that you have, except sin, in order to be with you, to cleanse you and give you life. Before your eyes is my Cross, on which I bore your sufferings and your sins, so that you might be cleansed by my grace."

Whoever believes in Christ is saved. Whoever calls on the name of Jesus and follows the Lord is saved. But to be saved, you must begin to follow Him. And in order to follow Him, we have to see that we are unworthy, that we cannot save ourselves and that first we must repent. We must take a truthful and honest look at ourselves. That's why we pray in the great canticle: "Open unto me, O Giver of Life, the gates of Repentance", for we are already used to things as they are, and the gates of repentance are closed to us. We think we are living normally, like everyone else, and sometimes, like the Pharisee in the parable, we take pride in ourselves and put on airs before others. But what do we have to be proud of? Today, in the Gospel reading, the Church bids us: 'Arise, like the tax collector, without thinking about your merits, your power or your good works. Just get up and repeat, as he did "Lord, be merciful to me, a sinner."

Amen.

The Tax Collector and the Pharisee

In the name of the Father and of the Son and of the Holy Spirit!

The festive days of Christmas have hardly gone before Lent is upon us. This is a wonderful time, which we all love - a time of repentance, when we start to sing that marvellous hymn of prayer "Open unto me, O Giver of Life, the Gates of Repentance". "Open", we ask, because it is hard for us to repent, to realise and sense our own weakness and poverty, our bankruptcy before God.

So the Church opens before us that precious page of the Gospel which speaks of two men praying: a righteous man and a sinner. The righteous man was a Pharisee, a devout man who obeyed the commandments laid down in the Law. He was confident that, whatever accounts he had to settle with the Lord God, he could already claim to have done all that was required and to have emerged better than other people. He prayed with a sense of complacency and pride. But where there is pride, there is also condemnation of others. Glancing at the tax collector standing behind him, he said "Lord, I thank Thee that I am not such a scoundrel as this man." He was bursting with self-righteousness, with his own superiority, and he stood, proud and complacent, before God. He may well have had something to be proud of: he had observed the fasts, paid donations to the temple and had committed no significant sins - he was, after all, an upright and righteous man! He stood before God, yet at the same time he was so far from Him; his soul did not move towards the Lord, because he was self-satisfied and contented. Even the words he uttered could be seen as pious: "I thank Thee, O God, that I am not as other men, extortioners, unjust, adulterers". He thanked God, as if he was aware that this was by God's gift, but he took pride in it, as if he had achieved it by himself.

The tax collector, however, had nothing to be proud of; he hardly dared to raise his eyes and took up a position somewhere at the back. In Old Testament times people prayed, not in the temple itself, but in the temple courtyard. So the Pharisee was standing at the front while the other man was somewhere by the gate, with his head bowed, just repeating "Lord, be merciful to me, a sinner". He was not seeking righteousness from the Lord, but only mercy. He understood that, where righteousness was concerned, he could not justify himself before God. We do not know what sins he had committed, apart from his abhorrent profession (he collected taxes on behalf of foreign conquerors), but he felt himself to be worthless, saying merely "God, be merciful to me, a sinner."

When the Lord Jesus told the story of these two men, He ended by saying "These two left the temple, but it was the tax collector, the sinner, who was acquitted of his sins, not the Pharisee, the righteous man". Perhaps we are surprised: how could it be - that the man who kept the commandments turned out to be far from God, while the sinner was justified and accepted by God? The point is that neither man could fulfil all the commandments, or wholly cleanse himself of any sin by his own efforts. There is also something else: a man who outwardly fulfils all the commandments, but retains pride, contempt and malice in his heart, will still remain far from God. God cannot be "bought off" by fasting or sacrifices, because - as the psalm tells us - "the sacrifice of God is a broken spirt" (meaning grief for one's sins), but "a broken and contrite heart God will not despise" and will not reject.

Once again we ask "What should we do then, seeing that the Pharisee's efforts were vain? Should we really stop

7

obeying the commandments and live anyhow, sinning as we please and then asking the Lord for forgiveness?" No, of course that was not what the Saviour had in mind when He told this parable. We must try, make an effort every day and every hour to wrestle with ourselves and with our sins, falling, rising, falling again and rising again, achieving something but remembering that tomorrow we might lose it again. We must fight, without weakening, but we must remember that, as far as righteousness is concerned, we are still unworthy and that the Lord accepts us because of His compassion. So we must not feel self-satisfied or proud. Someone who has come to a halt cannot keep moving towards God. If anyone says to himself "Well, now I've done all I need to do - I haven't murdered anyone, I haven't stolen, or disobeyed any other commandment, all is well with me" - that person will not come to the Lord. We must always sense that we are far from Him, always long to come nearer to Him, with love for the Lord inspiring us; we must try to go to Him even when we feel powerless, repeating the words of the tax collector "O God, be merciful to me, a sinner". We are acquitted, not through the Law, or by right, but through God's love. Our wish to come to Him meets His wish to receive us.

Through this parable we understand what the Apostle Paul meant when he said "Man is not saved (does not come close to God) through the works of the Law, but through faith - faith in the Lord Jesus Christ."

Once more I repeat - works are necessary, as are our efforts in the fight against sin, but we must never think we are perfecting ourselves through our own efforts alone. The grace of God, pardoning, forgiving and saving - that is our hope. We trust not in ourselves, but in Him. We struggle, but in the end everything depends on His salvation. And so we come to feel humility, which lives in our hearts, making us simple-hearted, modest and capable of seeing ourselves in the sober light of reality. In that humility and in that hope, let us now say again the tax collector's words, as the time of repentance draws near: "O God, be merciful to me, a sinner."

Amen.

THE PRODIGAL SON

In the name of the Father and of the Son and of the Holy Spirit!

In today's Gospel reading, we heard the parable of the Prodigal Son. In anticipation of each Lent, we repeat it once again, because this is a parable about God and man, about our relationship with our heavenly Father and with each other, about the Lord's attitude to us, as sinful and fallen human beings

You should know that at the time to which the Lord was referring, people tried to live as part of a family. Nowadays it is more normal for children to leave their parents and go away when they grow up. In those days however, people owned land in common, working on it together. The larger the family, the more hands there were to work and the more opportunity for work. So to divide a house, property or farming land was considered harmful and unprofitable. If children behaved like that, it was considered an insult to their parents.

So the Lord takes such a family as an example - a father and his two sons. One of them, the youngest, says to his father one day: "Give me my appointed portion of the inheritance - I want to live on my own." The father silently agrees, without reproaching his son - he gives him everything that is his due, although he could have denied him, for parents had the right to bequeath an inheritance or to refuse it. However, the father quietly hands it over and the son takes the money and journeys into a far country, where - through thoughtlessness and inexperience - he squanders it all, down to the last penny. His life was undisciplined and dissolute. He wasted the money, throwing it away on frivolous entertainment. Finally, before he knew it, he was

10

on the street - in rags, poor and homeless. In that country there was a famine and, as you remember, he became a farm labourer and looked after pigs. He was the son of a rich man, but had become a swineherd prepared even to eat out of the pigs' trough to satisfy his hunger. That was how he lived, plumbing the depths and becoming like a wild animal. Then suddenly he came to his senses. As the Evangelist says, "he came to himself" - and remembered. He thought "After all, my father's hired servants live better than I do. Of course, I shall be ashamed to appear before him, but I will go and say 'I am no longer worthy to be called your son. Just employ me as one of your labourers, so that I won't have to die of hunger in a foreign land."

That, then, was what he did and when he was getting near to his home, as the Lord says, his father saw him from afar. Note that it was as if the father had always been on the lookout for him, as if he was standing on the threshold waiting for his son, whom he still loved. He did not wait proudly, in order to reproach him, but sadly and lovingly. The old man ran to meet him first and embraced him and although the son said the words he had learnt by heart: "Father, I have sinned, I am no longer worthy to be called your son, I will be a servant to you", his father said nothing in reply. He led him into the house, ordered new clothes for him to put on and held a feast in his honour. Such was the father's joy. We can all understand that, as we all have children. But, although they often grieve us, to a mother or a father their children always remain their children, whatever they may have done. In this parable the Lord portrays these parental feelings. The father forgave everything. He said nothing and uttered no reproach, such as "Where did you lose my money?" Instead he held a feast.

At the same time the elder son, a respectable man, was coming home from the fields. He had not gone away

11

anywhere, or committed any sins. He had always been with his father. He was approaching the house when he saw that there were celebrations going on - feasting, noise, laughter, people singing and enjoying themselves. "What has happened?" he asks the servants. They tell him "It's your younger brother, who has squandered his share of the inheritance. He's come back and your father's holding a feast in his honour!"

"What sort of feast is this? I've always been with you and you never held even the smallest feast for my friends, but you've received him back when he threw away all he had on harlots - look how well you've treated him!"

Then his father said to him "My son, you are always with me and all that I have is yours. But we must rejoice about your brother, because for us he was dead and now he is alive again; he was lost, he had disappeared, but now he has been found; he has returned." So the Lord shows us what God's love for men is like.

Above all this parable is about our heavenly Father. When we say "I cannot be saved, I am worthless, there is no hope", let us remember that He is the One who is waiting for us, for we are all His children.

The parable is also about us, when we forget our heavenly Father, when we travel far from Him, carried away by our passions, by trivialities and by day-to-day life; when we are far, far away, a thousand miles from God and reality; when we live in our worldly way, squandering our spiritual treasures and all the gifts of the Holy Spirit. Then we are no longer able to pray, we cannot open the Holy Scriptures, because our heads are full of irrelevant thoughts and our hearts are vain and empty: those are the times when we fall away and lose touch, losing our way and at our wits' end.

It is also a parable about self-satisfied people - and therefore about us as well. After all, sometimes when you and I are assembled in church, we think "Well, we have come to church, but many people have stayed outside - bad, undeserving people. But we are deserving. They are impious, but we are religious. They are sinners, but we...well, perhaps we sin a little too...but all the same, we have pleased God, we have gathered here, we come here, we have not turned away from the Lord."

Now take a look at the elder son. He is always with his father, yet how unlike him he is! He could not be more different - because he has no love for his brother and feels no warmth towards him, nor indeed for his father. He is a self-satisfied, envious man. Perhaps you and I seem to be close to God? Here we are in church. We take communion, confess our sins and pray. Many of us say prayers every day and even read the Holy Bible, following the Church calendar. We are with God. But do we resemble our heavenly Father? That is what we should ask ourselves, for after all, we should resemble Him. Of course people are not necessarily like their parents, but in the spiritual sense they are free to take from them what they need. If anyone does not, it's their own fault.

So then, if we have one Father, the only Father of us all - our Lord and Creator - who is true justice, true righteousness, true love, goodness and wisdom, and if we ourselves do not possess these qualities, if we live a trivial, foolish and hate-filled life, then we are moving away from Him, leaving Him, and it is no justification that we are here in the same building with Him - we have nothing to be proud of or to boast about. See how the elder son seems to be reproaching his father, while stressing his own goodness. "I am always with you", he says, "I have served you faithfully, I have worked for you, so let's settle accounts". That's what we ourselves sometimes say: "Lord, why is it that I get ill, although I always go to church?" As if we come to the Lord, so that He can pay us for it later. That is not love for our Father - true love is unselfish.

So this parable reminds us of many, many things. We are now approaching the Lent fast, but in addition we are constantly approaching our own death. Today we have a dead man among us in church - the dead are with us almost every day. They remind us that, sooner or later, we shall also be lying here. In other words, our Father will summon us and we shall say "We have been far from you, we have learnt nothing and understood nothing, we have squandered and wasted everything". That is how we shall enter eternity - with empty souls, with no trace of the divine spark.

May it not be so! Let us try to make use of these days of repentance, when the Church calls on us to look back and come to our senses. We must not live like this any more! We must not live as if we were asleep! We must seize hold of life, and begin to live as true Christians. If it seems to us that we are not succeeding, that it won't work, that we are not strong enough and that it's all useless - let us remember our heavenly Father, who stands and waits and who will accept everyone that says from the depths of his soul "Father, I have sinned against heaven and in Thy sight."

Amen.

THE LAST JUDGEMENT

In the name of the Father and of the Son and of the Holy Spirit!

The last Sunday before Lent has acquired the name of Last Judgement Sunday. This pre-Lent feast, which we are accustomed to calling Shrovetide and which has been a period of merry-making since ancient times, coincides with an even older Church tradition - that of reading the Gospel passages on the Last Judgement and meditating on the Last Judgement.

The Lord said that He had not come to judge the world but to save it. Nevertheless, since that time the judgement of the world has begun, and not only that of the world, but of each one of us. For the face of Christ the Saviour stands before our consciences like a living judgement. God is not like an earthly judge. He does not judge and condemn us inhumanly or soullessly, following the letter of the law. No, the love of God comes to us all, to the whole human race, and to each one of us individually - and when it does, something happens to us, to each person in a different way.

When a volcano erupts, burning hot rocks fly out of the fiery mountain, lava flows in a glowing stream - and suddenly there in its path is a river. The fiery red-hot rocks fall into the river and a sort of explosion takes place - all the water evaporates, sometimes in the twinkling of an eye. This is like the love of God which, as it approaches each of us, suddenly makes contact with the dirt and cold of a deaf and dumb soul - and an explosion takes place. Not because God has lost His temper - that only happens with human beings - but because the pure has met the impure, the sinless has encountered the sinful, and the result is a storm.

The Judgement began from the moment when the Lord

first called people, when He called us all into His Kingdom, but we did not go - through laziness, indifference or vanity. We felt that there were more important things than God's Kingdom, than living at God's side, in His love and according to His commandments. He, however, said "Repent, for the Kingdom of God is at hand". He says to us even now "Repent, it is at hand..." - which means that the judgement of this world is near.

We might be tempted to remember the past at this point - how temples were destroyed, how whole countries perished because they had turned away from God and broken God's law. But that would take time, and we might think that it was only the people of ancient times who were guilty of sin.

People often ask "Why did God permit so many atrocities, so much evil?" All that we have seen in our time - cruel tyranny, lawlessness, terror, murders, treachery, the camps, spiritual demoralization among people - the Lord knew and foresaw. The Holy Bible pointed out where the false road taken by human beings would lead. Nevertheless people took the wrong road - and now they are reaping what they sowed. That too is the Judgement of God, which - I say again - is not a criminal court or a sentence, but the moral order which the Lord has laid down for all times and for each individual. People have experienced much that is terrible and difficult precisely because they have turned away from the right path.

Let us, though, think a little about ourselves. When the Lord says "Now is the Judgement of this world", it means that Judgement applies to each of us. His love comes to us, saying "Live with me, work, be happy, pray and be active in life. If you are old, help anyone you can. Live by means of prayer. If you are young, use all your powers to serve other people." As our Lord Jesus said "What you have done to my brethren, you have done unto me." We live at the Lord's side through prayer, through knowledge of God's Word, through love of the beauty of the world and of human life and by increasing all that is good in an evil world and all that is bright in a dark world.

Nevertheless we often fall away, our spirits flag, we float with the tide, believing that to do so is normal. In reality it is tedious, grey, boring, debilitating and, in the end, sinful, as we are separated from God. And since we are far from Him, our judgement has come and we have become weak. Every day we are subject to the judgement of God. When you choose how to act, whether to go to the right or to the left - that is the Judgement of God taking place; when your conscience awakens, that is the Judgement of God; when it is your duty to act contrary to your desires, that too is the Judgement of God. Finally, when you have to endure trials, that is also God's Judgement - a blessed, merciful judgement, because He wants to forge us into His children and not leave us lying in the dust, rotting like yesterday's grass, like autumn leaves or litter that no one needs. For every soul is precious to the Lord and He wants to bring every soul into God's Kingdom even here in this life. But we resist, preferring to live with the greyness and boredom of our sins. Then we meet Him and want to run away.

I remember the words of St. Augustine. In his book "Confessions", he writes that when he was still a pagan, but already beginning to turn to God with his whole heart, he prayed "Save me, O Lord, save me - only not today, but tomorrow; today I shall live as I did before". We are all like that. We want to live without changing. But life is short. Think - soon our hour will come and so will our judgement. What is the point of thinking about the end of the world, when the end of our own world is upon us and tomorrow we may already have been summoned? All that attracted us and made us happy in life will disappear: ambition, pride, our outward appearance and every kind of worldly vanity - all of these will fade away, as if blown by the wind, and we shall be left naked before God. All that will remain will be what we have amassed in our souls.

And what have we amassed? Next to nothing - not even good thoughts and even fewer good actions...How then can we come to Him, when we have no way of reaching Him? - when we have gradually lost everything in the course of life. Seeing this truth and sensing the stern judgement of our own consciences, you and I must pray to the Lord today for mercy : "Lord, be merciful to us sinners, not according to our merits, not because we have earned it by our works (what kind of works can we boast of?), but simply because of Your compassion, Christ our Saviour - because You came to save us, dirty, lazy, selfish and covered with the dust of life: it was to such people that You came."

We have an ikon "The Saviour's Descent into Hell". He seems always to be descending into hell. He descends into the hell of our lives and our souls, in order to deliver us from them. That is our only salvation. As the psalmist says: "All the ends of the earth have seen the salvation of our God".

Amen.

LORD, WHEN DID WE SEE YOU NEEDY, OR SUFFERING?

In the name of the Father and of the Son and of the Holy Spirit!

Nowadays people often say that our world is fragile and could easily perish; perhaps that is what will happen and you and I will witness the end of the world. The forces of nature, which the Lord created, are surely blind forces, indifferent to good or evil. If they are allowed to get out of control, they could sweep away all living things. Before life or mankind appeared, these elemental forces had already come into being. They have no pity. When lava flows down a hill, it can crush a village or a town - together with their people and the buildings those people have constructed so diligently and over such a long period. A hurricane, as it comes in from the sea, can destroy hundreds and thousands of lives.

Living creatures are not like that. Hunters have often seen how a mother wolf will sacrifice her own life to save her cubs, how animals will fight an unequal battle with birds of prey in defence of their young. Wild animals can experience fear, joy, love and gratitude; they are not without feeling. Of course, their feelings are not comparable to those of human beings, but all the same we know that living creatures are capable of helping each other. When a fire rages in the taiga, all creatures try to save themselves and at such a time the wolf will run beside the deer without touching it.

There are many examples of animals and plants helping each other. However, you and I are human beings and the greatest sin against human self-respect is indifference; when we become like the elements - like cold rock, a devouring fire or dangerous water. This is degrading for man, who

19

is created not only with the power of reason, but also with emotions and feelings, enabling him to share the sufferings of other men.

The Lord tells us a parable about how each one of us will be judged. By what criterion, by what sign, does the King of Heaven divide all men into black and white - black goats and white sheep - as a shepherd divides a flock? What is His accusation against those whom He places on the left hand? It is that they were indifferent: "You saw me sick and did not visit me, hungry and did not feed me, you saw me suffering and did not help me." But to those standing on His right hand, He says "Come, ye blessed of my Father, for you comforted and helped me." And both the first and the second say "Lord, when did we see you needy or suffering?" He replies to them "Whatever you did or did not do for the least of my brethren, that is, your own brothers and sisters, you did or did not do for me." That is the basic law of Gospel life.

Note that the Lord says that the Judge assembles before Himself all nations and languages, which must include pagans and unbelievers, but each of us knows this law in his conscience. Each believer should understand that, if he remains indifferent in the face of evil and suffering, he thereby betrays his Lord. Those who do not know God would feel that they were betraying themselves, their consciences, or some higher truth - which shows that this is a universal law.

The Lord tells us "It's not enough just to utter the words: 'love', 'goodness' and 'kindness'. Love must be active, it must be made manifest in life itself." The Apostle Paul also says that the most important thing in our life is faith, which works through love - note that it works actively. It is not indifferent. In the parable of the good Samaritan, the priest and the Levite who were walking along the road and saw a wounded man lying on the ground were certainly believers in God, but they were uncaring men. They looked at the man who was calling for help and walked past without helping him. It is this kind of indifference that the Lord condemns, while He blesses the heart that responds to other people - that is the whole law of the Gospel.

So let us ask the Lord to give us strength; to put His divine seal on our hearts, so that we may not become indifferent, like water or rocks; so that we may be living people, responding to the sufferings and needs of those around us.

And there is something else. In the parable, people are divided into black and white. But in all of us can be found the two contrasting aspects - black and white, generous and indifferent. So division and conflict are going on in the same human heart. May the principle that is victorious in us be the white, bright, good and loving one, so that we may hear the voice of our Lord: "Come, ye blessed of my Father, inherit the kingdom prepared for you from the foundations of the world."

Amen.

Forgiveness Sunday

In the name of the Father and of the Son and of the Holy Spirit!

The time of Lent is getting near - a time of renewal, purification, and, above all, of preparation for receiving God's healing grace. We come to Him sick in soul, carrying on our shoulders the heavy rocks of our weaknesses, sins and personal unworthiness. Which of us does not know how weak they are? Do we not know that we have tried a thousand times to free ourselves from our sins, to shake them off? But they have stuck to us once again and once again we have been forced to walk with bowed shoulders, dragging the filth of our disgusting, black load.

The Lord tells us, however, that He is the only gate to the kingdom of purity and light. Only by turning to Him, by discovering the power of His grace through prayer, can you and I come to life, change, and be transformed. But we have to prepare for that - and now the Church gives us this wonderful time of Lent, which anticipates the joy of Resurrection.

This is no coincidence, for we must die, and die twice. First, we must die together with the Lord. What does that mean? It means that as He suffered to save other people, so we must bear our own adversities and the sufferings of our lives. Even if they are not very great, we must bear them as our own particular cross, as if dying constantly together with him. Secondly, we must die to sin. And what does that mean? It means that we must incline our consciences, lives and souls to see sin as repulsive. Of course, we shall still be tempted and sin will continue to demonstrate its power over us. Nevertheless we will be hostile to it, not friendly. We will not welcome it, nor readily allow it into our lives; we will resist it to the end, even though our powers are limited.

Dying in this way, through repentance and through bearing the cross, we approach the holy days of Easter. Those among us who are prepared, who have sincerely followed this road, will encounter the true grace of Christ. The Church does all it can to help us.

Today we were reminded of Adam's fall, of the sinfulness we have in common. For Adam is you and I. All of us have fallen away from God. We have all gone our own way. All of us are in a state of disobedience and self-willed error, and we are all facing God's mercy. However sinful we may be, if we want to change our lives, the Lord will grant us the strength to do so.

Finally, we have heard some very important words of Christ, which show us that our preparedness is in our own hands. The Lord Jesus said "If you want the heavenly Father to forgive you, then you must forgive those who sin against you." This is easy to understand isn't it, quite simple and logical? Can we really say "Lord, forget this, erase it, blot it out", when there is still hatred in our hearts, when we nurture and bear malice? Of course not. So today the Church calls on us to forgive each other. We cannot live with each other without forgiving, for each person is always at fault before others: a husband before his wife, children before their parents, parents before children, neighbours before neighbours. We are people, living human beings, and if we were unable to forgive one another, then the whole world would turn into a hell, a hate-filled chaos.

So let us begin today. Let us call to mind all the evil there is in our lives and leave it on the threshold of Lent. Of course, I know this is difficult, but after all it is God's work. It is the call of Christ, for whose sake it is worthwhile denying ourselves. "This is an auspicious time", the Church tells us, and we cry out in the psalmist's words "Open unto

me,O Giver of Life, the Gates of Repentance". "Teach me
how to repent, teach me to see my sins and do not leave me
when I realise despairingly how great is their number and
their power, how insuperable is the power of sin. At the
moment when I tell myself that I cannot find salvation or
forgiveness, that I cannot be healed, give me the knowledge
that salvation does exist; that it is now a gift to us from
Christ's spirit, from Christ the Saviour, who is invisibly
present and alive among us, who came into this world so
that no-one might perish but all have eternal life."

Amen.

Lent

The period of Lent proper spans over nearly six weeks up to the eve of Palm Sunday. From introspecting penitence, we now turn to concentrate and prepare for the events of Christ's Passion in the seventh week. This period starts with the commemoration on the first Sunday of the restoration in 843 AD of the veneration of icons, a "true" restoration of faith and practice after 120 years of fierce persecution by the iconoclasts, and is suitably called "The Triumph of Orthodoxy". Fr. Alexander refers to the visible magnificence of the Trinity St.Sergius Monastery (p.28) founded by one of the most influential and popular saints of Russia St.Sergius of Radonezh (d.1392) and now the foremost centre of pilgrimage and spiritual renewal in the country. It is situated some 40 miles North East of Moscow in the same direction as his own church of Novaya Derevnya.

The spiritual tradition of prayer in the monastries of Athos in Greece and one of their foremost leaders, St. Gregory Palamas (d.1359) constitutes the commemoration of the second Sunday while the third Sunday is dedicated to the veneration of the Holy Cross, our sustainer through the arduous lenten journey of intense prayer and abstinence. The fourth Sunday celebrates St. John Climacus, or " of the Ladder", an ascetic of the monastery of Mt. Sinai (d.649) who described a ladder of spiritual ascent through virtues. The fifth Sunday celebrates a woman ascetic, St. Mary of Egypt (5c) who lived for 47 years in the desert beyond the Jordan in total isolation and penitence, conquering every vice and temptation of her past dissolute life.

Six weeks have elapsed now since the beginning of the lenten journey (p.46). After the winter months, Spring is now engulfing us, and Fr. Alexander speaking on the day of the Raising of Lazarus on the eve of Palm Sunday refers to the central role of the Holy Spirit in human Life, quoting from the daily prayer (p.48):

> *"Heavenly King, Comforter, the Spirit of Truth, who art in all places and fillest all things, treasure of blessings and giver of Life, come and abide in us, cleanse us from all impurity and in thy goodness save our souls".*

THE TRIUMPH OF ORTHODOXY

In the name of the Father and of the Son and of the Holy Spirit!

The first Sunday of Lent is called "the Sunday of the triumph of Orthodoxy" - the triumph of the Christian faith. It is no accident that on this day we read the words of the Gospel concerning one of the Lord's future disciples who had doubts, but was told by another "Come and see." He went and saw the Saviour. What this experience was like, the Evangelist does not tell us, but the disciple immediately understood everything, saw with his own eyes and above all sensed in his heart that the living truth was standing before him.

These same words "Come and see" apply to the Church of Christ as well as to Christ's appearance on earth. When people ask us: "Where is this truth of yours then, and what is it?" - for many regard it as outmoded, unnecessary or dead - we reply to them "Come and see". Don't come and look at us sinners however, for we are bad witnesses to what is divine, but look at our Lord, at His beauty and His love towards men; His sacrificial love and His Cross; His teachings; His sufferings and His Spirit which is with us. Come and see the holiness of the Gospel, its unsurpassed power, which has conquered for hundreds of years - no matter how people persecuted it and tried to destroy it; it has always risen from the grave, as Christ himself rose from the grave, conquering death. That is why the Church says "Do not look, O man, at our sins but at our Lord and at the great saints of ancient times."

Today the Epistle listed the just men of Old Testament times: that great cloud of witnesses, who were precious in this world. These people endured persecutions, slanders,

27

banishment, torture and death, but that was the path they had chosen, giving themselves to the Lord. In their choice, Orthodoxy also triumphed, as it is present above all in true faith.

As the Epistle says: "Moses preferred to leave a palace, riches and learning, in order to stand together with slaves and lead them according to God's will." Kings, prophets, judges and righteous men, who were persecuted and wandered through the dens and caves of the earth - all of them chose faith.

Don't think that the Church's triumph consists only of its outward splendour. Of course, when you visit the Trinity-Saint Sergius Monastery, you see the beautiful cathedrals and wonderful ikons, you hear the marvellous ringing of the bells resounding over the surrounding countryside. All this shows the beauty and the triumph of our faith. Yet all of it is transitory and perishable, it can be destroyed by evil men and by time. The true faith and the Spirit of Christ however, cannot be destroyed.

People who live by the spirit, like St. Sergius and all the saints of the New Testament, are also a cloud of witnesses. We repeat again "No, friend, do not look at us, for we are weak and powerless. Look at these saints, who overcame torture, suffering, banishment and humiliation, who testified about God through their love for men, their devoted service, their great endurance and their holiness and closeness to God - there they all stand." In them, in our saints, Orthodoxy has triumphed throughout the world, always and in all places. We are taught by them because they are our examples and teachers, but above all we are taught by the example of the Saviour Himself. That is why the Epistle ends with these great words "Let us run with patience the race that is set before us, looking unto Jesus as the Author and Teacher of our faith." *Amen.*

THE SUNDAY OF SAINT GREGORY PALAMAS

In the name of the Father and of the Son and of the Holy Spirit!

The Church has consecrated the second Sunday of Lent to the memory of St. Gregory Palamas, patron of men of prayer and of monks vowed to silence, known in olden times as "men of silence" and "heroic saints". They tried to preserve silence in their hearts, withdrawing to distant monasteries on Mount Athos, which were cut off from the world by its cliffs and the sea. Many of the cave-cells where they once lived are still in use today.

Why do we choose to honour the patron saint of silent monks on this day during Lent? Because it is at this time that we need to remind ourselves of the importance of silence and of keeping silent.

What is our life like? It goes by in constant noise and bustle. The whole existence of modern man is accompanied by all kinds of noise. We live surrounded by hubbub. People, especially those living in towns, are always aware of noise: the roar of cars and of crowds. Doctors tell us that this is bad for people's health. But for us its significance lies elsewhere: it dispels our spiritual concentration - you and I are already unused to silence. Many of us feel uncomfortable if we find ourselves having to be quite for a moment. Our heads are always full of idle thoughts, so that we cannot simultaneously keep calm and quiet for a time...But how many unnecessary words we use!...All this confusion and fuss deprives people of the opportunity to look at themselves, to remember what is really important and to come to their senses. The hurly-burly continues to our very last breath.

Sometimes, when an illness stops us cruelly in our

29

tracks, chaining us to our beds and tearing us suddenly from the general bustle, we manage to be alone with ourselves for a while. At such moments we start to think: what have we been living for? Where are we running to? Why have we been hurrying? This noise in our hearts and thoughts and all around us - where is it coming from? Should we not have found ourselves, just occasionally a few minutes of inner calm and silence a little earlier? How can God's grace come to us, how can it shield or illuminate us when we are deafened and blind and don't realise in our hurry where or why we are hurrying, unconscious of the voice of God?

The voice of God always rings out in silence. If you want to hear it, try to snatch at least a few minutes out of the day. The Church has given us a rule for that purpose: to read a prayer for a few minutes and to think consciously about yourself and what you have been doing during the day. What will your next day be like? What is it all for? This is important, so very important...

If anyone wants to learn the will of God, let them seek silence...

If anyone wants to concentrate their thoughts and feelings, then seek silence, for our thoughts and feelings are in disarray; they do not obey us, and we live in constant confusion. But the true spiritual life of men and women takes place in a focused way. We must bring our thoughts and feelings together into a quiet centre in the depths of our hearts, so that a silence will ensue in which God will utter His word concerning us. If we do not force ourselves to be silent, to keep silence, if we remain in subjection to life's endless bustle, our whole lives will go by on the surface, without any real meeting with the Lord.

That, then, is why we should remember the monks of silence and why the Church calls on us to oppose idle talk, empty, worthless chatter, and misusing the gift of speech to our own injury. "Set a watch, O Lord, before my mouth, keep thou the door of my lips", the Holy Bible says to us. This is what we pray for, what we ask from the Lord. But He expects us actively to help ourselves, to desire God's gift - the silence of His quiet blessing.

Amen.

Arise, your Sins are Forgiven you

In the name of the Father and of the Son and of the Holy Spirit!

Today, on the second Sunday of Lent, the Church opens to us a page of the Gospel that we all know well, about the healing of the man sick of the palsy. The man sick of the palsy was paralysed, lying like one dead, and others carried him to the Lord. From the Holy Scriptures we remember that four men were carrying the sick man on a stretcher, but when they arrived at the house where the Saviour was, they could not get inside because the crowd was so dense. The tried to get in through the door but could not. Nevertheless they did not give up. They climbed up on the roof, taking the stretcher with them; they took the roof apart and let down the stretcher into the room. Jesus, seeing their faith, said to the paralysed man "Rise, your sins are forgiven you."

Have you ever thought what kind of people they were - those who carried the stretcher? After all, it doesn't say that they were relatives, or the sick man's children, mother, father or brothers. Apparently they were simply friends, possibly neighbours. They made the effort for the sick man's sake, not their own. Not everyone would have climbed onto someone else's roof, taken it apart and let the stretcher down on ropes. It was probably awkward and difficult - but they wanted at all costs to get through to where the Lord was. And He saw their faith in their efforts and exertions. The main thing He saw in them, of course, was their love for this man. They had taken a lot of trouble on his behalf, expecting and believing that he would be healed; that the Lord Jesus could save this man who was lying there like a living corpse.

Reading these pages, I thought about the way things happen in our lives. I remember someone who was also paralysed - you all know who I mean; he had a son and other relatives, but no one gave him any help. He used to lie there like a piece of rubbish, like a corpse or worse. Such things happen often in our life here. Not always in so dreadful, mean and humiliating a manner, such as when a son cares nothing for his own mother; often it is less obvious. Hearts can be cold, uncaring and insensitive. But these men we read about in the Bible were quite different. They wanted this man to be healed so much, that was as if they themselves were ill and longed to rise from their sickbeds.

So, my dear friends, we have before us a great example for Lent. What kind of example? That we can be saved and find the Lord in our lives only together, by helping each other, loving and forgiving, stretching out a helping hand. If that is how we try and live, God's hand, Christ's hand will be stretched out to us in response. That is because, at the same time that He is saving us from the abyss, He wants us to help each other. When we cannot help outwardly, through action, we can help through prayer. So our daily prayers for each other should not be just a list of names. But when you yourselves pray for your relations and friends, for people close to you and for those in need, pray properly, with the same kind of persistence as the relations or friends of that paralysed man used to try and get into the house, to reach the Lord.

There will be obstacles - you know what they are: our laziness, weariness and weakness. How difficult it all is! We feel as if we were carrying heavy boulders, rather than praying. But at the moment when you find it difficult to pray for those close to you, remember that it was probably not very easy to haul the stretcher with the paralysed man in it onto the roof. Those men were rewarded however: Jesus saw their faith. And if you and I overcome our inertia, He will see our faith - so that in the end we shall overcome all obstacles. The

Lord tells us "Knock and it shall be opened unto you", so be persistent in prayer.

Do we not all know how confused and weak people are, how everyday matters endlessly distract us and fill our thoughts and emotions? It's funny to think that we allow these same matters, silly trifles that we won't even remember the day after tomorrow, to fill our short lives which, you would think, we would treasure above all else. All this cuts us off from our Lord, shutting us off from heaven and choking off prayer, like smoke from a funnel rising and obscuring the light from the sun. And what is smoke? It is made up of tiny black particles. In just the same way, our sins and restlessness rise and obscure everything like smoke - so that our life ceases to be Christian and becomes vain and pointless.

Only a search for the Lord, a longing to touch Christ the healer, can give us victory. It is Lent now and we are trying to pray more and practise abstention more often. A small abstention from food is a tiny, microscopic offering to God. Let us try to pull ourselves together spiritually and this time let us offer the Lord a prayer for each other - not for ourselves, not for our own health, salvation or well-being, but for our sisters and brothers, for those who are dear to our hearts: offer the Lord a prayer for them today, as the Gospel teaches us. Pray for them, that their way may be blessed, that the Lord may keep them and come to meet them - then all of us will ascend towards the Lord, as if holding on to that prayer. This is the main thing - the rest will follow - but this is essential to our lives. Then Jesus, seeing our faith, will say to all those for whom we have been praying, and to us, for whom they have been praying: "My child, awake from your sleep and your sickness, from your palsy, your spiritual paralysis; arise, your sins are forgiven you".

Amen.

THE ADORATION OF THE CROSS

In the name of the Father and of the Son and of the Holy Spirit!

The first Christians greatly loved depicting Moses in the wilderness on the walls of their churches, because for the Christian Church he was the harbinger of salvation and of the New Covenant.

The Holy Bible tells us that, after the Israelites - led by Moses, God's prophet - had crossed the sea and escaped from slavery, they fled deep into the dry, terrible desert, which to many of them seemed much worse than slavery, oppression and forced labour. For days, weeks and months they walked on, over rocks, scorched plains and cliffs. The heat there is remorseless such as we here can hardly imagine. People were dying without water. There were no springs, not a drop of moisture; they had left the sea behind them, there were no clouds in the burning sky, and it was a long way to the Holy Mountain where they were heading. No one knew how far they had to walk, on their bruised and bleeding feet.

Suddenly a small bush appeared and near it flowed a spring of water. People rushed to it, tried to drink and immediately spat the water out - it was bitter, like sea water. Evidently, in these places salt deposits have existed so long that they render the water undrinkable - and this spring was named "Marah": bitter. The people wept from resentment, disappointment and despair. Picture the scene - hope had flared up: in the scorching desert it seemed as if there was fresh water, cool, rising from below the ground. But it had turned out to be bitter and undrinkable. Then the prophet Moses cast a tree into the water and held it there, and the water gradually became drinkable.

This act of reviving the spring, which was almost poi-
sonous, reminds us of another tree, which is planted in the
midst of our life - the tree of the Cross. Today we stand
before its image. The tree of the Cross changes the bitterness
of life into pure, cool and living water - the salvation that
comes from the Lord. Not without reason did He say that
there were many standing there who would see the kingdom of God come with power. The kingdom of God comes
through the Cross of Christ, through His infinite love, that
enfolds us all. The kingdom of God is peace, light and
salvation in Christ.

However, it is possible to stand next to the spring of
water and not drink from it, to walk beside it - and still the
waters of life will remain bitter, if we go on living in the same
old way: egoistic, vain, proud and condemning each other.
If we really want the waters of salvation to touch our hearts
and revive them, we must try hard to stop condemning
others and extolling ourselves. We must put an end to
hatred, malice and slander - to all that poisons our lives,.
Then we shall see the kingdom of God coming with power,
not sometime, somewhere, or after death, but here, in this
life. Then everything will speak to us of our Lord, bearing
witness to Him.

In the mornings, if you can find just a moment among
your normal everyday affairs to stand before Him, you will
feel Him looking on you with love and summoning you to
work. God's blessing is with you in your work every day of
your life. The kingdom of God, which is coming with
power, finds a home in our hearts, for Christ said ''This is
what the kingdom of God within us means: go and drink the
living water of God's kingdom.'' But we stand like the
ancient Israelites at that spring, and the water seems bitter to
us for we lack the strong faith that would transform the bitter
water into living water. The bitter water of a life that is

cheerless, boring and full of monotonous work flows away into the sand - and there is no ray of hope, no salvation. Depression, sickness, weakness, affliction, bitterness, coldness of heart and meaninglessness in life - these are *Marah* - the bitter waters of our life without the Cross of Christ.

However, if we have the Cross, and if we have faith, then everything changes: we are standing before Him every moment and He touches our hearts. Only then does prayer begin to resound, whether silent or spoken. It bursts from the heart in gratitude and rapture - because of the love of God, because the Lord is with us. You came to us and filled us with your grace; you visited us - the unfit, weak and unworthy. The living water of God's Word, of Christ's Cross, flows towards us, to restore and revive us and to give us the strength to continue our journey.

Amen.

SUNDAY OF SAINT JOHN OF THE LADDER
(ST JOHN CLIMACUS)

In the name of the Father and of the Son and of the Holy Spirit!

Today we honour the memory of St. John of the Ladder, who reminds us of the central orientation of the Christian life. You all know what ordinary life is like: its main direction is down - a descending line. A person walks on, losing his strength, his reason and his senses, and finally he loses his life. He merely lives through what he received from God, from his parents and from nature. Christian life, on the other hand, grows richer with time. Despite the fact that our flesh grows weaker, we can and must rise above it. St. John Climacus shows us the ladder that leads to heaven, so that in old age and illness a man can find great love and wisdom and discover great depths.

Even today you and I come and stand before this ladder and think: "Lord, we are standing on the first step - we have achieved nothing, made no progress, we have not succeeded in loving you; our prayers remain aimless, forced, as if we were just making ourselves pray. Forgive us, Lord, for being slack and confused, for losing our sense of direction; our inner spiritual life hardly exists, it's only just keeping warm, like a small oil lamp, an ikon lamp.

Forgive us, Lord, for not trusting you, for always worrying about what will happen to us tomorrow or after tomorrow, or what will happen to the world - it's just lack of trust. Lack of trust is, in its way, a lack of faith, a form of unbelief. Lord, forgive us our sins. Moreover, faith is really trust in God in any circumstances - both as our strength declines and, conversely, at the height of our powers and in our joy when we decide to give ourselves to the

Lord Jesus Christ.

Lord, forgive us for our wavering and inconstancy, for the times when the main thing in our lives was not you, but our own "self", our self-assertion. For the sake of a false self-assertion we are prepared to do anything - forgive us, Lord.

Just think, how like we are to autumn leaves, falling and disappearing. It is only in God that we find eternal life, only in Christ that we find true worth - otherwise we are like dust or smoke, vanity of vanities, weariness of soul and nothing more. Lord, forgive us sinners for being worldly and small-minded, too much concerned with our daily work; we are envious and condemn others. All kinds of trivialities and empty nonsense take up most of our lives, our thoughts and feelings. Forgive us, Lord, for not behaving as if we were in your presence. When we are busy with some ordinary activity, we seem to move away from God - we live like pagans, not as if we were standing before you. Everything should take place in God's presence: work, love, joy, sorrow, suffering, sickness and failing health. Religion should not be a separate function of our lives: 'in the morning I do my professional work, in the afternoon I spend time with my family and in the evening I pursue my religion'. This is not the right approach to take. Forgive us, O Lord, for separating faith from life.

Forgive us, Lord, for our immoral thoughts - slanderous, impure and malicious: often we see only the bad side of people and suspect there is worse, because we ourselves are like that. Forgive us, Lord, for our confused thinking and for often ending up in extreme despair. A certain atheist said "If you look at the faces of these Christians, you would never think that they believe such wonderful things". If we truly believe that there is meaning, that the soul is immortal, that God is good and has come to us, that Christ is living with us - do we really have the right to be depressed? St. Seraphim said "There is no way that we can be despondent", and we will keep to that.

Lord, forgive us sinners for our lies, our vain chatter, our laziness and inertia, our unwillingness to help each other, for our callousness, our concentration on ourselves and our isolation from others, for our egoism.

Forgive us, Lord, for our sins against our family and those close to us. We have not shown much love to each other - after all, that would require some effort, as people everywhere find life in the world outside stressful, and so let themselves go at home. That is where all the darkness within them comes rushing out. And whom does this affect? Our family and neighbours, even though it is just here that we should be most caring. But we cannot manage it on our own and never will be able to. Only the grace of God can free us. Otherwise - as you yourselves know - it remains a vicious circle. We have to keep loving our friends and relations, but we have to let ourselves relax at home as well - which is where the vicious circle comes in...

God's grace can do anything, so we must always ask for it. Lord, forgive us sinners for our inability to thank other people, as well as yourself, for our disregard of God's Word, our neglect of Christian duty, charity and compassion for others; for our failure to observe fasts and Church festivals - for not even thinking about these festivals when we are at home. What are festivals? Are they necessary? Certainly we need festivals, especially where there are children. Children should feel that Easter has come -not just springtime, but the springtime of the soul; that Palm Sunday is here - that it was not just some time two thousand years ago when the Lord rode into Jerusalem, but that He comes to us even now - the One who went to His Passion of His own free will.

Thus He alone, only devotion to Him and the Spirit constitute life - the rest is rubbish and decay. Lord, forgive us for so rarely thanking you for your great love. We could thank you through love for you and for our neighbours, but not only do we not love them, we treat those around us with dislike. Even strangers, people unknown to us, passers by on the street, seem odious to us. Not because people really are odious - people are of various kinds, always have been and always will be - but because we have something murky inside us, that leaches out and makes everything appear to us in dark colours. I have not forgotten that many of you live in difficult, straitened circumstances, that you are subjected to temptation. But things always were like that and always will be: life on earth was never a paradise. While the kingdom of God has not come with power and glory, the earth will always be a vale of sorrows - and we must acknowledge that clearly and honestly. "In this world", the Lord said, "you shall have tribulation. But be of good cheer. I have overcome the world." If He also overcomes the world in us, we too will feel completely different, for the darkness of this world will no longer oppress or reign over us.

Lord, have mercy on us sinners.

SUNDAY OF SAINT MARY OF EGYPT

In the name of the Father and of the Son and of the Holy Spirit!

On the fifth Sunday of Lent the Church celebrates the memory of St. Mary of Egypt, an ascetic saint who is an example of profound and sincere repentance, that bore good fruit.

She became a saint after being a great sinner, spending her youth in debauchery; she was a prostitute, a courtesan - a fallen woman in a large and corrupt Egyptian city. However despite her way of life, there seems to have been a divine spark in Mary's heart that drew her towards God. She did not understand that she was not living according to the law of the Lord or the demands of conscience. She felt that she was doing no harm to anyone.

One day, a big ship was about to depart for the Holy Land, carrying pilgrims and Mary decided to go with them. She had no intention of visiting the Holy Places or going on a pilgrimage. She simply wanted to have a good time with people who were travelling on the ship. In that mood she sailed and landed at Jaffa in the Holy Land, from where she set off for Jerusalem, together with a crowd of pilgrims.

Hundreds and thousands of people were moving towards the Holy Sepulchre, in order to worship at the site of Christ's Cross and the tomb where the most pure Body of our Lord was laid. Among them were merchants, princes, warriors, city-dwellers and peasants - people from various nations, who spoke many languages. This whole colourful, many-faceted crowd was heading for the Holy Sepulchre.

Any Mary went with them...but, when she came to the entrance, some force pushed her back and would not let her go in. At first, she thought it was merely the size of the crowd preventing her from entering, but later she realized that all those who had been walking beside her - both men and women - had entered the church while she was still standing outside. Ten minutes passed, half an hour, an hour - but some unknown force would not allow her into the shrine.

At that moment, everything in her changed. She realized that she was unworthy to cross the threshold of God's house, that the Lord had barred her way. From that moment her life of repentance began. She completely changed her way of life and remained in the Holy Land, to atone for her sins.

It might occur to us to ask why exactly the Lord should have stopped this particular woman in such an amazing way and why He does not stop you or me? Why did that crowd of people enter, among whom there were certainly sinners, and perhaps much worse sinners than this poor Egyptian courtesan, this prostitute? Perhaps she had ended up in that situation because of poverty or thoughtlessness. Why was she the only one to be stopped? Why did God choose her? If we think about it honestly, that force should have pushed each one of us back from the church threshold, we who are equally unworthy to enter because of our sins.

Life gives no direct answer, but we can make a guess at what happened and why she was chosen. It must have been because that unfortunate, ignorant, loose-living young woman had a great soul. The Lord picked her out and stopped her, in order to awake her conscience. She wanted to come and bow before the Lord's tomb in all the simplicity of her heart, which was pure in its depths, although it had been corrupted. She asked nothing of God, but only wanted to come and stand at the site of His Golgotha. Obviously, thousands of people came there to pray - some for health, others for riches or success in their work, or for their children - each person has his own needs. But she did not ask for anything, she only wanted to come closer to the Lord and it was the fact that she was not allowed to that so upset her.

From that we should deduce something important: although the Lord himself tells us "Ask and it shall be given you", it is far less important to ask God for gifts than to ask that He Himself - His power, His grace and His love - should be with us.

In the Gospels we read that shortly before the Crucifixion, two disciples who imagined that the Lord was heading for glory and honour asked Him to give them places on the right and left hand of His throne. If they had sensed what the Lord was enduring at that time, when He was approaching the place where He would undergo His sufferings, they would not have asked such a question. But they were trapped in their own thoughts and desires, so they did.

Don't we act in the same way, when we stand before the Cross of Christ, just asking the Lord to grant our needs? Each of us knows that at times when we have no particular needs, when all is well with us, our prayers start to cool: we have to force ourselves to get up and pray. On the other hand, in desperate situations, when we are ill or in difficulties, when we endure trials - well, "when there's a thunderclap, the peasant crosses himself". So, as it would appear, only necessity moves us to prayer. In other words, if everything was just fine, if the Lord gave us all the gifts people usually dream of - health, success, happiness in family life and at work, would we then not even bother to pray? Perhaps we would just thank Him coldly and unconcernedly and quickly forget about it? Yes, sometimes that is what happens, and we all know it from bitter experience. That's the way things are...

However, Psalm 26 - "The Lord is my light and my salvation: whom then shall I fear?" - says of those who sought the Lord Himself, that they no longer have need of anything on earth. The essential thing is to love the Lord God with all your heart, all your mind and all your strength. "Seek ye my face", the Lord says, through the Psalmist. In other words, seek not only the gifts which I give you, but seek Me. Love of Christ is the foundation of our spiritual life. If it is not present, we shall be like the pagans, who go to their gods to obtain their daily necessities.

Our prayers must be purified from the desire for gain. Asking for something, as a child asks its mother, is the right thing to do. But as we know, children love their mothers. They reach for her hand, but not just because she holds a gift, or something they need. Children reach for their mother because they love her - she who bore them and carried them in her arms.

It is in just that kind of way that we should pray! Not only should we see the Lord's hand bearing gifts and reach out for it, but we should reach out for the Lord Himself, who is always beside us, as if He were crucified before our eyes.

Amen.

Awake Thou that Sleepest

In the name of the Father and of the Son and of the Holy Spirit!

"Awake, thou that sleepest and arise from the dead, and Christ shall restore thee to life" - so sang the Christians in the first days of the Church's existence. This call is also addressed to us, because our souls are sleeping a deep, heavy sleep: a sleep of sloth, covetousness and sin. The Church says to us "May Christ restore you to life!" We shall rise, in other words not through our own strength, but through the power of Christ.

Lent is the time when we should listen to these words and finally wake up. Perhaps last year we slept - the days go by so fast: it seems just like yesterday, but a whole month has gone by; it seems as if a month has gone, but already a year has flashed past - life rushes onwards, but we don't notice time going by. Why don't we notice? Because we are dreaming, letting ourselves be carried by the current; because we are weak. But the Church says to us "Awake, thou that sleepest, and arise from the dead." Our souls must arise, for at the moment they are dead, eaten away by sin.

Sometimes, when walking in the fields, you see a man standing and waving his arms, but as you get closer, it turns out to be a scarecrow, put there to frighten birds away from the crops. It's a dead thing, with a hat, a shirt and a stick...That's what our souls are like - they seem to be alive, but on closer inspection, they have no life - no clarity of thought, no living faith, no good feelings; everything has become rigid, all is covered with ice. It is wonderful that Lent coincides with springtime, when "dead" trees start to come to life and the earth, covered with snow, starts to reappear. It is then that the Church's words to us ring out:

"Awake, thou that sleepest and arise from the dead, and Christ shall restore thee to life."

This is where we grasp the essential point of our faith. I once asked an old lady "Are you a believer? Do you belong to the Orthodox faith?" "Yes", she said, "I come and pray for my dead." Is that what our faith consists of? Of course we should pray for the dead, but even pagans remember their dead and so do people who are not believers at all. On Sundays and Saturdays, there are often crowds of people visiting the cemeteries - but do all of them go there to pray? That is not enough, it is not the essential element of our faith. What is essential? Whom should we ask? Who will give us an answer? That answer - clear and unique - comes from the lips of Christ; there is no other answer, all else is false - human error and human tradition. So what does our Lord tell us? What is the essence of our faith, which can raise us up, awaken and resurrect us?

When the scribe called Nicodemus wanted to know what the essence of Christ's faith was, he came to the Lord Himself. Nicodemus was worried that his friends might find out. He feared that people would gossip about him, so he went to Him by night and asked "How should I live?" The Lord answered him "In order to enter the kingdom of God, a man must be born from above - he must be born again." Nicodemus said "How can I be born again, when I am an old man?" Then the Lord told him that he must be born of water and of the Spirit. By water He meant baptism, joining the Church, while the Spirit is our faith - which receives the Lord's power.

Each of us should pray that the Lord will give us that Spirit, that new birth. "If a man is not born from above, he will not enter the kingdom of God", says the Lord; whoever does not feel the touch of the Lord's hand, will stand in church as if he were dead to the end of his days and will not hear God's voice saying "Awake, get up, arise, thou that sleepest". In other words, only the Lord our Saviour can give us life - through the power of His Spirit. To whom will He send this power? To those who want it, who ask for it and pray for it, those who cry out for it, which is why the Church asks everyone to "continue in prayer". Every day we repeat "Come and abide in us and cleanse us from all impurity". We ask this so that the Lord may come within us, cleansing us from evil. This is indeed the true Christian life, of which Saint Seraphim says 'The aim of our life is to discover God's power in our hearts. Are we weak? Yes. Wicked? Yes. Powerless? Lazy? Asleep? Dead? Yes, indeed. But the Lord will come, He will awaken those who are sleeping and raise the dead."

Amen.

Palm Sunday

In the name of the Father and of the Son and of the Holy Spirit!

A week before Easter, when the Lord rode into Jerusalem on a donkey, the people were glad and rejoiced. But He wept. The people had their own ideas, hopes and wishes, but the Lord saw their future and He had tears in His eyes. He wept over Jerusalem, saying: "You did not know the time of your visitation." These words should be very significant for us, as the Lord visits everyone. He knocks at everyone's door. However secret, however unnoticed it is in the circumstances of our lives, we hear the Lord's call in the depths of our hearts: "Come unto me, listen to my voice." Often it so happens that we don't know the day of our visitation. I remember that once I was talking to an elderly man, whose life was grey and dull, lacking in anything spiritual. He told me that once, in his youth, he was walking along a city street when a wonderful inner light seemed to dazzle him and he saw the whole world around him lit up by the presence of God. For him, there was no longer any barrier dividing the earth from heaven.

That was a call from God and a visitation from the Lord, but later, as he told me, it was all left behind and forgotten. Years went by, he was overcome by worldly preoccupations and cares, and never again did he turn to the One who had called him.

That Voice calls each one of us. Each of us, if we truly think back, will find in our lives such moments, when the Lord was very near and the heart was filled with a force that came from Him. But later we forgot, we abandoned it and plunged back into our tawdry life with its vanities - and the light faded. We walk once again along the road of life, with an inscription round our necks proclaiming that we are Christians, members of the Orthodox Church, but in our hearts there is darkness, gloom, depression, fear and hopelessness. We have not known the time of our visitation, we have not kindled the flame that the Lord brought into our souls. We must remember that, by listening carefully and looking out for God's signals, we should be ready to respond at any moment. When we are forced to choose how to behave - between a base, mean course of action or according to conscience - it means that we have been visited by the Lord. It is the hour of our visitation. It is our misfortune if we don't realize it. If we have to make a choice and find it difficult to overcome our inertia, our laziness and weakness; if we feel the need to open the Word of God or to pray, but have to rouse or force ourselves in order to do so and feel ourselves being dragged down as if by a stone - that is a sign of God's visitation.

Let us conquer ourselves and take a step in the direction of the Lord's call, otherwise He will withdraw and we shall lose the strength He gives us. When you are leaving church, remember those moments in your lives - whether difficult or joyful - when the Lord really looked at you, waiting to see what you would do next. Let us think what the future has in store for us. Let us respond to His call. What is this call like, you may ask, where is it? For us, it rings out always from the Word of God. If we delve into it, then the living voice of the living Christ will ring out from that Book, from the pages of Scripture.

St. Theodosius of the Caves, when he was a young man, often went to church. But one day, when he was earnestly listening to the Gospel reading, the words that were being read out struck him like lightning and changed his whole life. It was the same with St. Antony the Great, founder of monasticism, and many other saints and ascetics.

It was as if a light suddenly shone on them and the words they had heard a thousand times took on a new meaning.

So, my dear friends, you and I have not been abandoned; we are not alone or separated from God. He is beside us and walks with us along the road of our life. From time to time, in order to strengthen and support us, He turns to us with a rebuke or an appeal, or in expectation. And we shall try to detect His voice, to hear it, and not to let the day of our visitation go by.

Amen.

Holy Week

In Holy Week, the liturgy follow the classical Christian pattern: the Last Supper is remembered on Thursday; the Crucifixion on Friday; the Burial on Saturday, with its climax, the resurrection, on Sunday. One aspect of it, however, is worth emphasising: the notion of the Sabbath, God's day of rest, on Saturday. Lying lifeless in the grave, having accomplished the work of redemption, the Lord "is awaiting his hour". There lies the mystery of his Person as the Incarnate Son of God:

> "In the grave with the body, but in Hell with the soul, in that Thou art God; in Paradise with the thief, and on the throne with the Father and the Spirit, wast thou, O Christ, filling all things in that Thou art uncircumscribed" (from the Easter liturgy).

The icon of Holy Saturday is that of Christ's descent into Hell (1 Peter 3.19) already mentioned earlier in the sermon of the Judgement (p.18).

MAUNDY THURSDAY

In the name of the Father and of the Son and of the Holy Spirit!

When the Lord and His disciples assembled for the Last Supper, He told them "With desire I have desired to eat this passover with you". Why did the Lord want so much to be together with His disciples on this particular day? Since His youth He had always celebrated this holy feast, but that year He attributed special significance to the Passover. However, from His words and hints, they were able to understand that during these passover days, He wished to establish a New Covenant and proclaim the kingdom of God. It was because of this that the authorities, having found out from Judas where Jesus was, were in a hurry to capture Him - despite the feast, the large numbers of people around and the possibility that the people might rise in revolt. They were afraid that something might happen at this Passover, that Jesus would do something that might shake their authority and the old establishment. His enemies were in a hurry, but the Lord waited. As He had once said: "I have come to send fire on the earth". He waited in holy impatience for the fire to flare up.

Now the evening of Holy Thursday comes and we see - as if with our spiritual eyes -the Lord bringing together the disciples He loved most, in order to establish the New Covenant in His blood. A covenant implies closeness, kinship, agreement and unity. So in ancient times, when a covenant was concluded, all those present were sprinkled with the blood of a sacrificial lamb. Why blood? Because blood is the symbol of life. "The power of life," according to the ancients, "is in the blood". That meant blood was sacred, as it united all parts of the body. When the blood of a

53

sacrificial victim was sprinkled on all those who took part in a religious service, they became as it were of one blood - that is, one life. They were united by the power of the Lord. The Lord was present, though unseen, during this kind of Old Testament sacrifice. So the Lord Jesus chose this ritual of the Old Covenant to found His New Covenant.

When He spoke of His blood, He was speaking of His life; when speaking of His flesh, He was referring to Himself, incarnate in the world. When He said "Take, eat" and "Drink ye all of it", He wanted His power, His life and His divine and human nature to become one with us, so that the links of the eternal covenant might unite us with Him and with each other.

As people who have drunk from the same cup and eaten from the same table communicate with the essential power that maintains their lives, so in the same way the Sacred Cup represents the descent of God's Spirit, the power of Christ. Every time that this Cup is raised in a church, the Last Supper takes place again. Once more the Lord is here, unseen, together with us, and He says to us: "I died for you, I came into this beautiful world that I created, which has been darkened by your sins, by the influence of Satan. I shall die here, because what is holy must inevitably perish when darkness comes. This is my sacrifice of love - being with you in spite of death, in spite of the sin which is my burden today." Thus He is the Lamb of God, who takes on Himself the sins of the world.

Once there was an ancient ritual: priests put their hands on a sacrificial animal, laying on it all their sins and offering the animal to God, with great repentance. Now there is no sacrificial lamb, but there is the God-Man - Christ and His love, who takes it all upon Himself, absorbing in Himself the sufferings of each one of us. And on this night, when He was having a meal, waiting minute by minute for

His enemies to appear, He thought not of Himself but of each of us. He gave Himself for us.

This holy night, made dark by the treachery of Judas, is the night when God descends into this world. What does He encounter? - the weakness, fear and betrayal of His disciples. He also encounters the indifference of the crowd, the cruelty of His executioners, the injustice of His judges - all the evil of the world, turned against Him. Everyone was either against Him or had abandoned Him. He drank the bitterest of cups that night, in order to ransom and cleanse us.

Today we approach the sacred table once again, praying "I will not give Thee a kiss like Judas" - because each of us could betray Him, like Judas, who came up to Him and asked "Is it I, Lord?" The Lord is silent, though, because He reads in our souls how often we have mocked His law, disobeyed and insulted Him and so helped to crucify Him.

Because of this, we approach the sacred Cup feeling as if we are unable - or forbidden - to drink it and that it is only because of His grace that we dare to come to His table, to the Last Supper. So may this day and this Cup remind us that being near the Lord can end either in salvation - or, as with Judas, in destruction. Light can blind a man. Today we have been granted a great mystery. If we do not use the power of holiness in our lives, it reacts against us and our souls fall into darkness. Being together with the Lord means having a great responsibility, being weighed in the balance of His justice, resolving to believe in His love and giving Him all we possess.

So, in coming up to take the Cup, we must repeat these words over and over again: "I will not give Thee a kiss like Judas, but trustingly say, like the thief on the cross: "Lord, remember me in your kingdom."

Amen.

GOOD FRIDAY

In the name of the Father and of the Son and of the Holy Spirit!

The last Gospel of Christ - St. John's Gospel - describes the Lord's trial, His sufferings, death and burial. Throughout three short years, the Lord had preached every day. As St. Mark tells us, sometimes He and His disciples didn't even have bread to eat. He spoke and did a great deal. John the Evangelist says that if all the things He said and did were to be written down, the world itself could not contain the books that would be written.

However, when He stood before unjust judges, Christ was silent. This is mentioned by all the evangelists. He answered the high priest only once and then was silent. When He was ridiculed, beaten and mocked, He was silent. When He was brought before Pilate, He also answered Him briefly and then fell silent. What did this mean? Why was He, who formerly inspired people with faith and hope now keeping silent?

It was because He had already said all He had to say and also because His unjust judges would have remained deaf to His words and His defence. That was the reason for His silence. Only once during the trial, in answer to the question "Art thou the Christ, the Son of the Blessed?" did he reply "I am", adding "and you shall see the Son of Man coming in glory, in the clouds of heaven." He said this and once more fell silent. Then, when He was dying, those standing around the Cross heard only a few words from Him. He suffered and died in silence. How many bitter words He could have found for the ungrateful human race. But He was silent, for He was the God-Man, through whom the Lord revealed Himself to us. He had said everything, taught everything; He had opened the doors - and thereafter He was silent. He submitted to insults, ingratitude, flogging and death.

Is it not the same in our lives? We sometimes feel that the Lord is silent, that He does not respond to our sufferings and sadness, to our sorrowful prayers. In fact,however, He is listening. He knows and feels for us, just as He did then, at the time when He Himself was suffering. He suffered when He stood before men blinded by envy, hatred and malice, yet was silent because His heart was moved even for them - for their degradation, their sins and blindness. In the same way our Lord suffers for us, seemingly without speaking. We appeal to Him, but we must not think that His divine silence signifies indifference, that He "doesn't hear", as we say. He cannot fail to hear. It is simply that, as before, He has already told us everything. He has said more to us than the world or our hearts could contain. He has shown us the road to life and now He is silently awaiting a movement of the heart or will in each one of us.

In the same way that He broke His silence then, and spoke of the Son of Man coming to judge the living and the dead, so now the Lord tells us that He is long-suffering. He silently endures our sinfulness, our meanness, our lack of faith - all our unworthiness - but not for ever. A time will come when all will be weighed by the justice of God. For us, the silence of the Cross is both a reproach and a call to a real Christian life. Most important of all for us is the fact that He acknowledges us, for we know that the One who was silent on the Cross, who is silent in heaven, is also the One who is our Saviour, who has not forgotten or left us. He is our only hope.

Amen.

HOLY SATURDAY

In the name of the Father and of the Son and of the Holy Spirit!

We human beings are not merely God's creations but God's children - cherished, chosen, loved beings. Although of course the Lord loves the whole world, the whole universe that He created, we human beings are special among His creation, for we alone have the right to call ourselves God's children, created in His image and likeness. In order that this image and likeness might impress itself on us even more, the Lord Himself gradually came closer to men in order to unite with them. That would have been the great triumph of love, a great triumph for mankind, for all creation. The Creator Himself coming to men! What could be more wonderful than that He should unite Himself with them: beings not perfect, but beautiful?

But of course, that is not how it all happened. As the Epistle reading tells us, instead of finding the joy that was His due, the Lord Jesus endured suffering. This was because He came to men and found them other than as the Lord had intended. As a result, His encounter with us, His incarnation and His life among us became for Him a Cross - suffering and death - when He came into contact with our sickness and evil. That is why the Cross stands before us, why the Lord's Tomb is now before us. He who should have been reigning and rejoicing with us lies lifeless today, murdered by our sins and our wickedness.

Nevertheless this is not the final death, because the Lord who is awaiting His hour stands before us. He died like everyone else, like millions of others. He breathed His tortured last breath on the Cross, was buried and the tomb was closed. But we wait and not in vain - because the justice and power of God cannot be overcome by our evil. So we cry out, as in the psalm "Arise, O God and judge the earth, for Thou shalt reign over all nations." The Lord rises, in order to raise us; He conquers death, so that death may have no dominion over us.

Amen.

How Simon of Cyrene carried the Cross

In the name of the Father and of the Son and of the Holy Spirit!

A man's fate is sometimes astounding. Long, long ago, many centuries ago, there lived a devout farmer. He lived in the town of Cyrene, in Egypt, in the Jewish settlement there. He had two sons, Alexander and Rufus, and he himself was called Simon. One day, we don't know why, he called his family together and decided to set off for the land of his fathers, to the city of Jerusalem. He travelled there, found and bought a house for himself, as well as a field near the city, where he worked together with his sons, so feeding his household and himself. It was an ordinary life, an ordinary calling - there were hundreds, thousands, hundreds of thousands, of such people, of such farms and settlers.

However, it is no chance that this man, Simon, has always been remembered by the Church. It so happened that on the eve of that Passover Friday in April he had gone to work in his field: perhaps he had been tending his vinetrees. Then, early in the morning he was returning home to prepare for the Old Testament Passover festival. At that point he ran into a dreadful, sombre procession: crowds of idle onlookers and impassive, unfeeling soldiers who were leading criminals to their execution. Each of the three condemned men had been forced to carry a heavy wooden beam: stooping under these beams, in chains, they were going towards the city gates, to the old stone quarry, where they were to be executed - by being crucified on these cross-beams and left to die of thirst and loss of blood.

As Simon was about to pass the gloomy procession, he noticed that one of the men no longer had the strength to carry his burden - the heavy cross beam. No matter how the soldiers struck him with their swords, he could not take another step. Then one of the soldiers went up to Simon, seized him roughly by the arm and said "You carry it." It was useless to resist and instead of returning home, Simon lifted the heavy beam onto his shoulders and walked beside the men condemned to death. While he was walking in this dreary procession, it certainly did not occur to him that, from that moment, he had become the bearer of the Lord Jesus's Cross, that by carrying His cross-beam he would stand together with Him on Golgotha and share His burden.

We do not know what happened afterwards, because Simon's name is not mentioned again in the Gospels or in any other part of the New Testament. However, we do know that his sons, Alexander and Rufus, were Christians and later were well-known in the Church.

Maybe, after that agonizingly terrible moment when Simon took the heavy Cross on himself, he came to know the truth and came to know the Saviour also. When he saw his God beside him, humiliated, covered in bloodstains and the bruises caused by the blows, a crown of thorns on His brow - for that was how he saw Him, in the lowest human state of degradation - how could be not be appalled and recoil? Yet this was our Lord, our Saviour, because He had taken on Himself all the sufferings of the human race. Sin too He had taken on Himself, though He was without sin.

Simon of Cyrene was the first to obey Christ's command, when the Lord said "Whosoever will come after me, let him deny himself and take up his cross". This means : 'share with me my sufferings for the world : share with me my longing - as the Heart of God - to suffer together with the world, to die for the world and revive the world'. Simon of Cyrene was the first to do so and the Lord calls us to follow him. Let each of us carry his burden, his work and his sorrows, not just patiently but as Simon bore it, sharing it with the Lord. There is a reason why we all wear a cross - it means that we must serve the world and mankind and serve God and our Lord and Saviour.

The terrible sign of the cross is at the same time a sign of joy and of victory. That is why we adorn it as we do, for the cross became not only an instrument of execution, a gallows, but also the instrument of our salvation. So let us not leave our Lord alone on the cross. After all, He had with Him both Simon, who carried the Cross, and the thief who repented. May our small crosses be beside His, so that we may suffer with Him, rejoice with Him and with Him possess eternal life, eternal love and the undying sun of truth.

Amen.

From Easter To Pentecost

Christ's resurrection is a token of the coming reign of God. The Scriptural readings prescribed for this period show the transforming effect His presence had on those people who came in contact with him. In his sermon for the second Sunday after Easter, Fr. Alexander adds the historical examples of a few holy women who contributed to the manifestation of the reign of God in their own times. Two queens are remembered: first St Helena (d.330), the mother of emperor Constantine; during her first visit to Jerusalem, she is known to have caused the finding of the holy and lifegiving Cross on which Christ was crucified. The princess St. Olga (d.969) grand-mother of prince Vladimir, the baptizer of Kievan Russia; she was instrumental in the advent of Christianity in her country. St. Juliana (d.1604), mother of a large family; through the practice of many virtues she set an example of Christian concern for those surrounding her. St. Xenia of St. Petersburg (18c), recently canonized: through her prayer she cured people of their illnesses and performed other miracles. Fr. Alexander also mentions Mother Theresa of Calcutta and Mother Maria (d.1945), an exile Russian in Paris who helped a multitude of those in dire need and rescued many Jews hounded by the German army of occupation; this caused her being sent to Ravensbruck where she died a martyr's death.

The ritual of the blessing of holy water is familiar to church goers (p.72), as holy water is frequently blessed in the Russian Church for the use of priests and people.

The Old Believers (p.76) are members of a schism within the Russian Orthodox Church which occurred in the 17th century under Patriarch Nikon; hence their referring to the official Church as "Nikonians".

Pentecost is celebrated twice, as it were, in the Orthodox liturgy. On Sunday, the final revelation of the Holy Trinity is settled, while on Monday, the Third Person, the Holy Spirit, the one responsible for the final revelation, is venerated in a personal way.

The last Sunday, of All Saints, can be considered as part of Pentecost in that the company of All Saints commemorated are in fact witnesses of the Holy Spirit, and this Sunday may be said to be an extension of the feast of the outpouring of the Holy Spirit by a further week, and beyond - to the remainder of the year.

A TALK FOR EASTER

In the name of the Father and of the Son and of the Holy Spirit!

When you and I turn to the Holy Scriptures and read about those radiant days when the Lord appeared after His Resurrection, let us reflect on something very important which we may not all have noticed. He appeared to many people, but to each of them in a different way. On one occasion it was the weeping Mary Magdalene, grieving alone by the empty tomb; another time it was Peter, confused and troubled after returning from the garden, where he had found the stone rolled away from the tomb. Later we see the disciples on the lake. John senses the Lord's presence in his heart and recognises Him; Peter plunges in at once and swims to Him. Then, as we read in the letters of the Apostle Paul, among the last people to whom the Lord appeared was Paul himself - or Saul, who used to persecute the Church of God.

This continues even now. The risen Christ is unseen, but manifests Himself perceptibly to each of us. Any one of us who in our lives has sensed, even for a moment, the proximity of another world has had an encounter with the risen Lord. He comes to everyone, knocking at the door of their hearts and find His own words for each one. Our task is to listen, to respond to that knock, for the Lord has come to save, revive and change the lives of each one of us. So on Easter Day, as we return to our homes, may each of us take that joy away with us in our hearts; along with the thought that the Lord has manifested Himself to me, He has risen for my sake as well. He speaks to me, He remains with me and always will - as my Lord, my Saviour and my God. May the Lord preserve you.

Christ is risen!

The Sunday of Saint Thomas

In the name of the Father and of the Son and of the Holy Spirit!

Today is the Apostle Thomas's day. You remember that the Lord appeared to him in a special way. Ten of the disciples were together when the Lord, having conquered death, came to them and said "Peace be with you". These were precious words. He brought peace into human souls, that peace which also comes to us now. He stood talking to them and sent them out to preach the word of God. However, one of them, Thomas, was not present. When he arrived, the others all rushed to him, saying "Brother Thomas, we have seen the Lord, we have seen Him alive, we touched Him!" Then Thomas felt such pain in his heart, felt so hurt that he said "I don't believe it, I don't!" (even though ten people - his brethren - were telling him so). He declared "Unless I touch His wounds with my own hands, unless I feel His newly resurrected body, I will not believe it."

Some time later the disciples had met again, locking the doors from fear of persecution, when suddenly a familiar voice rang out again, the voice of Jesus: "Peace be with you!" And there He was, standing among them. The first to whom He turned was Thomas. Jesus said "Thomas, give me your hand, touch my wounds, verify them and make sure." But of course Thomas did not try to: as soon as he saw the Lord, he was overwhelmed and fell before Him in tears, crying "My Lord and my God!" Jesus said to him "Because you have seen, you believed. But blessed are those who have not seen and yet believe."

Whom is He talking about? Why, you and me. We did not see the Lord during His earthly life, but we see Him with our spiritual eyes. He is alive amongst us and we have no need to touch Him. How many saw Him with their own eyes, heard Him speak, followed Him along the streets - and did not believe, because their hearts did not respond to Christ's call. We, however, have responded. Though we are weak and powerless, though we are very different, we have come to the Lord saying "My Lord and my God."

It is true that we seem to sense the Lord's presence, as everything around us is from Him and all of it is His. I remember a scholar who spent many years studying flowers, trees and herbs - all kinds of plants and animals. He made notes on everything and drew up long lists, which even now, thirty years later, are used throughout the world. Finally, when he had finished his work with the list of living things, he said "God has been near me. I have sensed Him in His creations." Indeed, the sun above us is the eye of God, the wind's breath is God's voice, all the laws of this world are God's laws, all the reverses and changes of our fate are also from the Lord. We see and sense Him in prayer, in the Holy Scriptures and in the sacraments. When the sacred Cup is brought to us - it is the real and living Lord who is present here, in this church, as He is in all the churches of the earth. He is present not only in churches, but in all the places where people pray to Him - in the far North, in deserts and in the mountains, as well as in populous towns where millions are crowded together: everywhere there are souls turning to the Lord. They see Him and feel His presence, for they are a hundred times happier and more blessed than those who lived two thousand years ago. The Lord is with us here, living, resurrected and giving us His blessing - and we, together with His apostle Thomas, bow before Him, saying "Lord, you stand alive before me, my Lord and my God."

Amen.

THE WOMEN WHO BROUGHT SPICES TO THE TOMB

In the name of the Father and of the Son and of the Holy Spirit!

Today is the feast day devoted to the women who brought spices to Christ's tomb, and also the day when we honour the memory of Joseph and Nicodemus - two Pharisees, members of the ruling council, who were responsible for burying the Lord. It is the day on which we honour loyalty, for these people alone remained true to the Lord in those first days. Nicodemus and Joseph believed Jesus's message but because formerly they had been afraid openly to express their faith in the coming kingdom of God, they used to come to Him in secret. You remember how Nicodemus came to Him by night, so that his colleagues would not see that he was visiting the hunted teacher.

Is this not how many of us often come to the Lord, ashamed of the fact and hiding it? I still remember a scene I witnessed many years ago. It was far away, in Siberia, at Easter. That night the church was full to overflowing with people all around it. A professor from a college had come and was standing, like the tax collector, at the back of the crowd. With his collar turned up and his hat pulled down, he crossed himself timidly, glancing about him. His soul was reaching out to the Church but he was afraid. Can we judge him? After all, if someone had caught sight of him there, he would certainly have run into difficulties and complications and might even have lost his job.

Nicodemus must have come by night in the same way. Joseph of Arimathea, who occasionally spoke out in the Saviour's defence against His enemies, was also His secret disciple. They maintained their loyalty to Him through the worst moments of mourning and despair, when all the disciples had abandoned the Lord and fled. Joseph and Nicodemus, risking their reputations, went to Pilate and asked his permission to bury the body of their executed teacher. The bodies of executed criminals were usually thrown into a common grave, but Pilate granted them permission and, as we know, it was Joseph and Nicodemus who carried the Lord's body to the tomb, which was in a garden.

Meanwhile the women were looking on from afar. They did not dare to come too near. They on the other hand, had been at Golgotha, where few of the Lord's closest friends had been. The women who stood there supporting the Virgin Mary are almost unknown to us. We know their names: there was Mary from Magdala (Mary Magdalene), there was Joanna, wife of Chuza, Herod's steward, as well as Salome, mother of the apostles James and John, and some other women from Galilee. They stood on the hill of Golgotha and watched their Lord and teacher dying. They saw where His body was placed and agreed among themselves that after the Sabbath, on which buying and selling were forbidden, they would buy spices, anoint the Lord's body and say their own prayers of mourning (for Joseph and Nicodemus had been able only to say hurried prayers before sunset).

It is amazing that it was to these women that the Lord appeared first, appearing only later to Peter and the others. That is what the Evangelists tell us. It is true that the Apostle Paul says He first appeared to Peter, but by this he meant that Peter was the first among the apostles to see Him; Paul simply does not mention Mary Magdalene. However, as you know, the women were carrying what was necessary for burial - "myrrh" - which is why we call them the spice bearers, and they were the ones who saw Him first.

This was the joy of victory and of faith which had shown itself strong in adversity. It was easy to be faithful to the Lord on the day of His triumphal entry into Jerusalem, when all the people greeted Him, rejoicing and praising Him. But to remain faithful to Him on the day of His shameful death - that was true loyalty.

It is the same with our own faith. It is impossible without loyalty, because the circumstances of our lives and the state of our souls and bodies change. When you are in despair, sick or suffering, when you lose heart and are full of bitterness, when you have a grudge against the whole world - to remain loyal to the Lord then shows true faith.

Today we also honour all saintly women, as today is a blessed day for Christian women. Look at the whole assembly of them: mothers, wives and brides, nuns and virgins, princesses as well as nameless wanderers and fools in Christ. Women could serve Christ's Church in various ways and still can, for they are called to God's service through the Mother of God, who is more worthy of honour than the Seraphim.

When the Lord was visiting Martha and Mary, He said that they should not worry only about housework or always be in the kitchen, preparing food; He said that Mary had chosen the better part, as she had been listening to His words. They all listened to His word: the martyrs, who laid down their lives for the faith; the queens, like Helena, who was "equal to the apostles", or Princess Olga, both of whom were converted and then helped to convert their subjects to the faith; good mothers, who had throngs of children, like St. Juliana Lazarevskaya, a wonderful person who saved the starving from death in the difficult years of Ancient Russia. She was indeed a mother to many.

Recently we celebrated the canonization of the Blessed Xenia. She is not so well known in Moscow and is honoured more in Leningrad - in Petrograd, where there is a chapel named after her. I myself have seen many people go there to thank Saint Xenia for healing them. Healings were witnessed there. In one authentic case a lame woman came and was led round the chapel three times but the fourth time she walked round on her own two legs. It was not the only such case.

Christian women serve the Lord and have always served Him. Not long ago our church here was visited by some nuns from India, who have formed a charitable order, a sisterhood of mercy. What do these girls, women and elderly women own? All the property they possess is a mattress, a small pail in which they put their toiletries and the white robe - an Indian sari, in which they travel everywhere - and that's all. Just the things that are absolutely necessary. They devote all their strength and the love in their hearts to the unfortunate, the sick and dying, the victims of various disasters. Anywhere on earth where there has been some disaster, these sisters of charity are always to be found. They are led by Mother Teresa (or Tarasia, as we would say), an elderly woman from Albania, who has given her whole life, first to the poor of India and later to those of other countries.

We honour the memory of Mother Maria, who lived in exile in Paris and died in a German concentration camp for trying to save those persecuted by the fascists.

These women are real heroines - the saints of our time. In speaking of them, I simply want to show that the great services rendered by women were not just part of sacred history but continue today - and remain possible for us and for you women.

Today we greet you all - mothers, grandmothers, wives, sisters and daughters - on this your day of Christian women. May the Lord bless you and give you strength to serve the Spirit of the Gospel and the Truth.

Amen.

THE CRIPPLED MAN

In the name of the Father and of the Son and of the Holy Spirit!

We usually read today's Gospel reading at the Blessing of the Waters, so its words are well known to us all. The Lord Jesus had come to Jerusalem and went to the so-called Pool of Bethesda (the Sheep Market), a miserable, dirty place, where the sick, including many pagans, lay. To this day pagan inscriptions, thanking the gods for healing them, are preserved on the walls of this pool. From time to time the water in the pool was disturbed and people would crawl in, swearing, pushing and shoving each other out of the way, for whoever got in first benefited from the water's healing power. The harder it was to get to it, the more everyone made a great effort to do so. This was a terrible place - a place rent with, envy and hatred, with quarrels and the moaning of the sick. Most people tried to avoid it. There were five porches, dug deep into the ground; steps led down to them on various levels. Everywhere lay the sick, groaning, contorted and foul-smelling.

The Lord Jesus came to this kingdom of sorrow to share people's sufferings with them. He looked round and His eye fell on an old grey-haired, paralysed man, who lay there without moving. The Lord went up to him and asked "Have you been lying here long?" He replied "Thirty-eight years - all my life." All his life...he must have been supplied with food by well-wishers. Someone else must have turned him over; at other times he would have lain there like a corpse. But he could find no-one to drag him into the water. His only hope was that a day would come when he could be one of the first to plunge his body into the water and his sickness would leave him. The Lord had said to him "So you've been

72

lying here a long time..." "Thirty-eight years...I have no one to help me." Even if he himself had summoned all his strength and crawled down, he would have been overtaken by others, who would have pushed him aside just the same.

This was the lowest level of human degradation: he had lain there like a stone in that foul-smelling place all his life, abandoned by everyone, sick and lonely. Suddenly he heard the voice of Christ the Saviour speaking to him. He did not know who it was that was questioning him, he responded as if in a dream, half conscious. The voice said to him "Rise - rise, take up your bed and go home." As if in a dream, he began to get up. He began to feel life returning to his arms and to sense his legs. The man got up, not really understanding what had happened to him, but he automatically began to pick up his bed, without saying "thank you", without thanking God. He took up the mattress on which he had lain, rolled it up, put it on his shoulder and began to walk home.

But the Lord Jesus knew what sort of man this was; He knew that his soul was not beyond reproach. As the cured man was walking home, dragging his mattress, pious people who encountered him said "Today is the Sabbath day, how dare you carry anything!" According to the law of God, he should not have done so. He replied "The man who healed me told me to do it and I did." "Who was it who healed you? Who could have broken God's Law on the Sabbath?" "I don't know," he said, "I didn't see his face." Later the Lord met him in the temple and said "Sin no more or you may suffer something worse." The old man looked at Him and recognized Him, and went and declared that it was Jesus who had told him to break God's law on the Sabbath. That old man betrayed the Lord, enabling Him to be condemned and slandered once again as others said: "See how he teaches people to break God's law".

73

It is this incident that the Evangelist describes to us today. Immediately we imagine ourselves lying there, in our sickness and our sins. Everyone knows there is only one who is able to heal us - and if He stretches out His hand to us, we shall not be ungrateful to Him. He has become a living source of healing water for us. Think of that pool, where the water acquired healing properties only now and then, but still desperate people threw themselves into it. We have another pool - the Word of God, the undying fountain of life, the Holy Gospels and the Holy Bible, which contain all that is necessary for the life of man. Our fountain is the sacred Cup to which we come, along with our prayers and our life in the Church. This source is renewed not once a year, but eternally - anyone can come to it at any time. Just touch it, desire it and come close - and you will feel its healing power.

When the years bow our backs, when all that darkens our lives - partings, afflictions, insults, injuries and disappointments - lies on our souls like a stone; when grief, depression and the empty greyness of our lives eat away at us; when we truly resemble the dying, the paralysed and the incurably ill, let us remember that we have one Name, the dearest name - that of Jesus, which raises, heals and revives us.

Amen.

The Woman of Samaria

In the name of the Father and of the Son and of the Holy Spirit!

This Sunday is called "the Sunday of the woman of Samaria" and it is a day consecrated to that Hebrew, a Samaritan. Why has she been given such an honour? Who was she, that a special Sunday is devoted to her? It is because of a conversation which the Lord had with her - a marvellous conversation. Everything that the Evangelist tells us about it, every word of it, is a treasure.

First we see the Lord walking under a burning sun. At last He grew tired, worn out from the hard journey along a stony path and He sat down by a well. Picture our Lord, to whom all natural forces and worlds should be subject, walking along like an ordinary traveller and, like them, bearing the hardships of life - heat, thirst and weariness. He is doing this in order to share our fate, to be closer to mankind, to find us on the roads of life. Then He has this chance meeting by the well - with a woman from a Samaritan village, who had come down the path to the well with a pitcher on her shoulder. Did she have any idea whom she would find there at the well? She was probably not thinking about anything, just walking along, suffering from the heat, carrying a water-vessel on her shoulder, as was the custom. She knew that soon she would draw up the water and then have to drag herself up the hill again in the heat. She was remembering her unhappy, ruined life: five times she had attempted marriage and every time it had been a failure; whether it was her fault or that of others, we do not know - but she was bitterly unhappy.

She came up to the well, a very old stone well; according to tradition, it was already over 1500 years old and many generations had drunk from it. A traveller with a staff in his hand was sitting there; He was dressed like a Jew and spoke like one. He said to her "Give me something to drink." He asked for a drink because the well was deep and she had a water-vessel on a rope. She knew, though, that there was a centuries-old hostility between the Jews and the Samaritans. So strong was this that they considered it shameful to drink out of the same cup. This is like our relations with the Old Believers - they don't drink together with the 'Nikonians', that is, with us - the Orthodox. When I used to visit Old Believers in the taiga, they always gave me a separate cup - it was called the "pagan's" cup, although it was kept clean and ready for guests. So for this same reason, the Samaritan woman was surprised - "How is it that you, a Jew, ask for a drink from my water-jug?" But He said to her "You gave me this water, but I shall give you living water; once you have drunk this water, you will never thirst again." She decided that this was some kind of spell, perhaps it was really magic water - once you had drunk it, you never needed to drink again. So she said "Lord, give me that water, and then I shall not need to keep coming all this way."

He saw that she did not understand. He was talking about a different kind of water - spiritual water. He then decided to approach her in another way. He told her "Go, call your husband". She said "I have no husband". "Yes," He said, "You have had five husbands and this one is not your husband." She realised that He knew about her sad life and her lonely fate. Clearly she was an exceptional woman, for she immediately forgot about her request that He should give her some magic water and launched into a conversation about problems of faith: which faith was the correct one? "I see, sir," she said, "that you are a prophet. Explain to me which faith is correct. You Jews pray to God in Jerusalem, but we Samaritans pray on our mountain, Gerizim. Where is it

76

right to pray to God, here or there?"

To this the Lord replied that the law of God from ancient times had certainly enjoined prayer at Jerusalem. "For salvation", He said, "is of the Jews." But the time was coming, when it would not be important where men pray - on this mountain or on that one, because God is everywhere and His love is everywhere, His heaven is everywhere. We must worship Him in spirit and in truth. The true faith is not the one that is linked with one place or another, but the one that exists in spirit and in truth.

What does that mean? To worship the Lord with your whole heart, through love and devotion to Him, and by doing good - that indeed is the spirit of truth. That is the kind of faithful worshipper that God wants.

The woman did not understand this very well. But neither have millions of other people, including educated people and theologians. How can it be: if there is one law here and another there, then one must be true and the other false? But the Lord says "Only one thing is true: love God and love man - all the rest will follow."

The embarrassed woman said "Very well, the time will come when the Saviour appears. He will tell us all things.". She thought that time was still far off, that it would come some day, perhaps after a thousand years. Then she heard His reply - the wonderful, simple words: "I am He, I who am speaking to you."

She did not ask Him anything else, but turned and ran back along the path to her village. What was she thinking about? Her first thought was of her fellow-villagers, people who were dear to her and among whom she lived - she wanted to share the joyful news with them. In one moment she had come to believe that before her stood salvation and the true Word of God. She was not a theologian and was probably illiterate, but her heart had begun to beat and she had felt the presence of God and she ran back.

Meanwhile the Lord sat by Himself, meditating - who knows what about? Possibly about the woman, or the Samaritans (by the way, they live there to this day; there are about 400 of them left), about human fate, or religious conflicts and wars - what He was thinking about, we do not know, we can only guess. But His face was joyful.

When the apostles came up to Him - they had gone to buy food - and said "Master, have something to eat", He replied "I have had enough to eat, I have other food". They began to look at each other: could someone have come to the well and fed Him? But He said "No, my food is to do the will of my Father."

At that point, they heard shouting and a motley crowd of Samaritans in vivid white robes came down to them. The Samaritans surrounded the Jewish traveller, not caring that He was from a hostile nation, and led Him into their village; we do not know what happened then, but the most important thing in this story is the result. After listening to Him, they said to the woman: "Now we see the truth; no longer because of what you said, but because we have seen for ourselves."

So now all of us are in the same position: at first we believe in the words written in the Scriptures and in other books, then we believe in what other people tell us. But the happiest moment in our spiritual lives is when we come to know the mystery of God, the mystery of the Lord Jesus, as revealed in our hearts, no longer through the words of others but through our own instincts and our own profound experience. We, like the Samaritans, guess at what is true and ponder on it. But He is near us, He reveals His word to us. Only we must also be ready to hear Him - like that simple woman of Samaria, like everyone who has ears to hear and hears.

Amen.

THE ASCENSION

In the name of the Father and of the Son and of the Holy Spirit!

During His earthly life, Christ the Saviour loved to withdraw to the hills, where the sky seemed closer and wide expanses of the earth were visible. In the desert, when He was tempted by the devil but resisted all his temptations, He seemed to be standing upon such a high mountain that from it He could see all the kingdoms of the world. It was on another mountain that He prayed and His face shone and His clothes became white as light - that was His Transfiguration. He often stayed there with His disciples and often passed the night there also. The mountain was not far from Jerusalem and it was there, on the threshold of His suffering, that the Lord spoke to His disciples about the future of the world, of mankind and of Jerusalem.

After He had appeared to the disciples, He climbed with them up that same Mount of Olives. We do not know if it was morning or evening, but from there, from the hill top, the hills and valleys unfolded before them and the city lay below them: Jerusalem, the home of righteous men and sinners, prophets and murderers, kings and priests. Perhaps the Lord stood in the same place where He had foretold the future of the world. Sending out His disciples from there, He said "As the Father sent me into this world, so I send you." They stood there: timid, joyful, unsure of themselves, not knowing what the future would bring. One of them asked "Lord, perhaps you will now restore the kingdom to Jerusalem?" They did not know where He was sending them or why. Later, however, they were enlightened by the Spirit of God, and God's Spirit showed them the way and gave them the power of the Word.

For the time being, the Lord raised His hand and blessed them, blessing at the same time all those whom they would later teach, and all their descendants; all those hundreds, thousands and millions of people. "All power is given unto me", He said, "in heaven and on earth". Formerly He had been subject to our human laws. He needed food and water, sleep and rest. But now He had overcome it all, He had conquered even death. It was after the Resurrection that He said "All power is given unto me in heaven and on earth". Everything is now flowing towards Him. The whole world will gradually become subject to the Risen Lord - not in an hour or a day, not in a century, but over time all will be subject to the Lord Jesus.

When He had blessed them, a cloud hid Him from them. This cloud has still not disappeared. We do not see Christ with our physical eyes, but He remains here on earth. He is on earth as well as in heaven; He is both God and Man; He is eternal and He is also with us in our short lives; we can touch Him, we can hear His voice, because the Lord is with us.

That is why the Church sings the words of the anthem: "Thou hast ascended into glory, Christ our God, giving joy to Thy disciples". What kind of joy could it be, when they were parting from Him, when He would no longer be appearing to them in visible form? The joy was because He would remain with them for ever, and with us, with each person who loves Him, because He is the Saviour who came into a sinful world to save sinners, of whom I am the first. The joy of being with the Lord for ever - that is what the Ascension means. Now He is no longer in Jerusalem, nor in Bethlehem, nor in Nazareth - not on a mountain or in a valley, by the sea or in a city, but everywhere. He has taken His place at the right hand of God. He is where God is, and God is everywhere. So in any part of the world, at any time of the day or night, we can always call upon Him and He will be beside us. He will hear us, because He is with us all our days to the end of time.

Amen.

THE SUNDAY OF THE HOLY FATHERS

In the name of the Father and of the Son and of the Holy Spirit!

Today you and I remember the First Ecumenical Council and the Church Fathers who attended that Council. Why should we remember those events of days long past? After all, the First Ecumenical Council took place in 325 AD, over sixteen centuries ago. However it is important and valuable to us, because the First Ecumenical Council defended throughout the Christian world the central truth of our faith - a truth that is not just a matter of the intellect, but is the focus of our salvation, of our life here and now.

In those days there were many theologians who expressed their views on the mystery of God, something that the human mind is unable to grasp. Nevertheless the searching mind of man has tried to penetrate even that inaccessible mystery. Human intelligence has often conceived all kinds of doubtful opinions and false teachings. One of these shook the whole Christian world of that time. It was called Arianism, after Arius, a presbyter from Alexandria in Egypt. He said that, although Christ the Saviour was indeed divine, He was not the Supreme God but one of the great beings created by the Supreme God.

Don't forget that at that time the population of the Roman Empire consisted in the main of pagans, or of former pagans who had recently become converts. At their level of understanding there were many gods in heaven and on earth. They imagined gods in charge of the stars, the winds, the seas, the forces of nature, the plants and the animals.

Now Arius was saying "Yes, we glorify Jesus Christ; yes, we worship Him, we call Him by the name of God. But that does not mean" - he said - "that the one who lived on earth in the form of a man, who suffered, rejoiced, grew sad or weary from travel, who Himself bore all weaknesses except sin, is the same Supreme Creator, who made everything. He is like a lower god, second in rank, a created being."

With such theories, Arius' views gradually spread far and wide and people found his teaching sensible and easy to understand. The true, supreme God was indeed beyond our comprehension, while Christ, who had lived on earth, was like a small god, created for us by the Heavenly Father. If the holy Fathers of that time had not realised how dangerous this doctrine was, the whole of Christian doctrine would have become fundamentally distorted.

What does the joy of our salvation consist of? Of the fact that it was not an angel, or some higher being, but the Lord Himself who descended to become one of us. It was the Lord who gave Himself, so that man might be united with His divine life. The Apostle Paul teaches us that it was no power, no heavenly being, no authority, no principality, no angel, but the God who is absolute ruler everywhere who became man on earth for our salvation. It is He who gives us the power of grace. He is the one who loves the human race - each individual soul and all of us together.

So when St. Athanasius and the other great Fathers of the Church at that time defended and fought for this truth, challenging Arianism, they were defending what is most precious and true to us - without which there is no real Christian faith.

When you and I turn to the Cross, on which Christ our Saviour was crucified, we know that God is suffering together with the world in order finally to lift us out of this vale of tears. His heavenly love has come down to earth. He endured suffering, although it was alien to Him, endured it along with us and lived through it all, even the death agony and death itself. This is what we hold dear.

But is this simply wish fulfilment? - is that why we cling to it so? No, we say this not on our own authority, but on that of the Word of God. Because it is in God's Word, in the Holy Scriptures, that this truth - and no other - is revealed.

So today, when we honour the memory of the Fathers, we read in church the words our Saviour used in His prayer as high priest: they make it clear to us that all those doctrines were false, that the Lord Himself, with His loving heart, came down into the world. This is what the Lord Himself says: "This is life eternal, that they may know Thee, the only True God, and Jesus Christ, whom Thou has sent." Eternal life, in other words, is already ours to receive. We can know, here and now, the True God, the One who came from within God, who is the Word of God - Jesus Christ.

When He was on earth, He glorified the Father, by showing us His great power. "I have glorified Thee on earth, I have finished the work which Thou gavest me to do...I have manifested Thy name to the men which Thou gavest me...Now they have known that all things whatsoever Thou hast given me are of Thee...All mine are Thine and Thine are mine, and I am glorified in them. Holy Father, keep through Thine own name those whom Thou hast given me, that they may be one, as we are".

One, as we are! So says Christ - man and God-Man, mortal and immortal, divine and earthly - when addressing the Heavenly Father, with whom He is one. That is what the unity of the Father and the Son means. These words of Christ also contain an appeal to us, to each of us: "May they all be one, as Thou, Father, art in me and I in Thee." So the mystery of the Holy Trinity, which we shall be glorifying and praising in our prayers next week, is not for us some distant, abstract theory, but the living Word of God, given to us for this life. Everything I have mentioned has been given us as a great gift, to nurture and sustain us every day, every minute, every second of our lives. All that the Church reveals to us, everything in the Holy Scriptures - all these great mysteries - are related to life. So try to explore their meaning, try to understand them with your hearts, as well as with your minds. Then you will see that none of the dogmas confirmed by the Ecumenical Councils was handed on to us merely to satisfy our curiosity, or so that we might know something new. Everything has been given to us for life, for life here and now, because Christ wants our life here already to be part of eternity and has opened up the way for this to come about. "May they know Thee, the only true God, and Jesus Christ, whom Thou hast sent!"

Amen.

THE DAY OF THE HOLY TRINITY

In the name of the Father and of the Son and of the Holy Spirit!

The Easter days ended, but nothing changed. If you and I had been near the house in which Christ's disciples used to meet, what would we have seen? Locked doors and people hiding behind them. They had not yet rid themselves of fear, nor had anyone heard of them. They were sharing the joy of faith among themselves. It was as if there was a small light burning inside their houses, which could not be seen from outside. The disciples and some others had received joyful news.

Let us remember, however, who these disciples were. They were of course proud men, and naturally they were seeking their own good. They had tried to apportion their places in the future, when the Lord would come in glory. Naturally each of them sought to be in first place. They argued about who would be first. When the Lord was foretelling His own death, Peter said "Lord, this will never happen to you" - because he was thinking in human terms, not God's. "Many, many times", as the Evangelist tells us, "they did not understand what Jesus said to them." One of them lacked understanding to such an extent that he lost his faith and betrayed Him. The disciples are weak, powerless and sinful; they take a step forward and then draw back; they walk on the water for a moment, but then start to drown. Peter even denied the Lord on the very night of His Passion. He denied Him three times.

That was what the disciples were like. To us it is a consolation, for we see how the Lord formed His servants out of such clay and dust. By touching them, as if with a magic staff, He transformed them into apostles - on the day of

Pentecost, which we are celebrating.

The doors were closed, the disciples were hiding inside. All of a sudden there was a noise like that of thunder or a stormy wind, the windows burst open and they all fell on their knees, while a vision of tongues of fire appeared above their heads. A flame rested on each one of them. And these weak, frightened men fell to the ground and became Christ's apostles. On that day, when a large number of people had gathered in Jerusalem, they went up on to the roof and from there began fearlessly to proclaim the word of God. "Men and brothers", said the Apostle Peter, the same man who had denied the Lord, "Jesus of Nazareth, whom you crucified, has ben raised from the dead by God - of which we are witnesses."

Everything was forgotten - all their fear and weakness. Moreover, there was such power in their words that thousands of people believed their testimony. So powerful was it, that it went even further and reached as far as you and me. Just imagine! If the Spirit of Christ, the Holy Spirit, that proceeds from the Father, had not been sent down that day, if He had not been sent to the room in which the disciples were meeting, then they would not have gone out and carried the word of God and of the Gospel to us - and we would still be in darkness.

The same process happens to us. After all, we too are weak and sinful people, perhaps far more sinful than the apostles were at the beginning. When we turn to Christ, we are seeking above all for peace in our souls, food for our minds and certainty in our lives; we are seeking this for our own sake, as the apostles did. But as the Lord did not reproach or reject them, so He does not reject us either, in spite of our egoism, because He awaits the conversion of our hearts.

Until Pentecost, until the Descent of the Holy Spirit, the

apostles were only potentially Christ's disciples. Afterwards they became disciples in reality. You and I are also only potential disciples of Christ, potential Christians. So far we have been more like the disciples before the Resurrection. However, the Lord sends His Spirit to us as well and if we choose to receive Him, we shall see our former selves and the life that we were leading. For that to happen a transformation must take place in our hearts. We must abandon our spiritual sleep. The Spirit of God touches us but we are not aware of it. The thick walls of our dwellings do not let the light in, the thick walls of our hearts do not allow the rays of grace to penetrate and we are crippled, as before, as if the Spirit of God had never touched us. We drag into the Kingdom of God the long line of our sins, the heavy burden of our passions and weaknesses. There is nothing in us that could have been born of the Holy Spirit. We must check to see if that Spirit is in us - but if He is not, we are not real Christians.

The Apostle Paul describes how he visited communities of believers and asked "Do you know what the Holy Spirit is?" They replied "We have never even heard of it." You and I can say that we have heard of it, but we don't know it; we have read about it, but we don't know it. Perhaps we know with our minds, but in reality He has not touched us, because we ourselves did not want Him to. We must take a step forward - then the Lord will say to us what He said to His disciples: "I am sending you out -all of you, all believers - as the Father sent me. I am sending twelve disciples, seventy disciples, five hundred, a thousand - all of you. I am sending you: bear witness to my Truth throughout the world, for I want all men to be saved."

Instead we say "Lord, how can you send us out? Are we suitable witnesses for you? We can only discredit your teachings and the title of Christian." But the Lord says "Yes,

I know and I see it. Nevertheless I am sending you, so that you will not think you re doing it all by your own power. My Spirit will be proclaimed by weak and fragile vessels and through your unworthiness." Be ready to receive that Spirit. Try constantly, day and night, to cleanse your hearts, because they must become the temples of the Spirit.

A temple must be adorned. You and I have adorned this church with green branches in honour of this festival. We must adorn our hearts too, so that the fire of the Holy Spirit will descend on them. If the temple is not ready, the Lord will not come; if it is not decorated, the Spirit will not enter. And if He does not enter, our house will remain empty. Therefore on the holy day of Pentecost we shall not just say "Come, Holy Spirit and dwell in us, come to us" - we shall also say "we want to be ready to receive You. We want the temple of our souls to be ready. We don't know how to. We can't. But we want to. Teach us how to do so and give us the power to encounter You and to be ready for Your baptism of fire, of which we are not yet worthy."

Amen.

The Day of the Holy Spirit

In the name of the Father and of the Son and of the Holy Spirit!

When the temple guard, the soldiers who used to keep order in the House of God, were sent by the temple authorities to seize the Lord, they returned without success, as they had not been able to lay hands on Him. When sternly asked: "Why did you not bring him back with you?" - they replied "No one ever spoke like this man." There was power in the words of Christ the Saviour. But that power was not there in the words of His disciples, because the force that spoke through Him was divine, while human weakness alone spoke through them. Even when the disciples had seen the Resurrected One with their own eyes, they hid in fear, locking their doors. Despite everything, they did not believe. They doubted, even when they saw Him on the mountain in Galilee, as the Evangelist Matthew tells us. Some worshipped Him, but others doubted, believing it to be a ghost.

A few weeks later, on the feast of Pentecost, everything changed. Less than a month had passed since the Lord had died at the place of the skull, in full view of everyone, and then risen again, showing Himself to be faithful and true. Suddenly there was a great noise of troubled voices - and Christ's disciples came out of the house and bore witness to the Risen Christ in front of a whole crowd of people. Everything in them had changed: their fear, timidity and confused speech had gone, as if they had never existed. They spoke so that everyone could understand, even visitors from distant lands who did not know the language well. Their words were now reaching everyone. Why? What was happening? They were able to bear witness because the divine power of the Lord had descended on them - not in a human way, not through flesh and blood, but directly through the Holy Spirit; so they could openly say "This Jesus, God has raised from the dead, whereof we are all witnesses."

This is an important saying, which we should take to our hearts, like those witnesses. Every Christian is a witness for God. Think for a moment what a witness is in our ordinary life. In court, a witness must describe truthfully what he has seen and heard and tell what he really knows honestly and truly. There are false witnesses and slanderers, but a true witness speaks only the truth - and not just the truth, but a truth that he knows well personally. So the power of Christian witness lies in what we say about the Lord whom we know, about the grace we have experienced, the blessing that is ours and the faith which is in our hearts. If we do not have that Spirit, that power, then we are bad disciples.

The apostles said: "He has been raised by God and we are the witnesses thereof" - because they knew it, they had seen it with their own eyes and had experienced it. But what about us? When we pray to the Lord after taking Holy Communion, do we not touch Him? All true faith is contact with the Lord, but once there has been living contact with God, with the Risen Christ who has saved us, it means we can honestly and courageously witness to the world about our hope, our consolation and our joy.

Our joy is the Lord, who loves the world, trying to save each man and seeking every soul that has erred. We do not say this just because of reports by others. We ourselves must be witnesses of His Spirit and His power. Let us pray today for the most important thing of all - that the Spirit of the Lord, which is promised to us, to each one of us, should come to us and touch our hearts. Then we shall say, not in vain, but out of the experience of our hearts, that we know our Lord and have known the touch of the Spirit of Christ and of God. Then we shall have the right to say "Yes, we know Him, whom we have loved, who has loved us, saved us and given us the gift of eternal life." To Him we all cry "King of Heaven, Comforter, Spirit of Truth, come and make your home in us."

Amen.